Cook Family Ancestors

Elias and Ballie Cook Family

Compiled and edited by Joni Wilson

Copyright © 2022 Joni Wilson and Susan Barnes

All rights reserved.

Personal photos and images used with the permission of
Joni Wilson and Susan Barnes.

Some images from US government records. Public domain.

ISBN: 978-1-7333158-4-5

Gracious Lily Publishing

Cover photo: Elias and Ballie Cook with their six children, circa 1894, Tennessee. Left to right: Tera, Eric (front), Heber (back), Elias (father) holding Gela, Ballie (mother), Berber, Irma.

Disclaimer

Most of the information contained in this book was acquired through online sources, primarily Ancestry, which was made available at no charge to Mid-Continent Public Library (Missouri) users.

While every effort has been made to verify the information, there are limitations. Not all records are currently available online. At the time of this writing, US Census records were only available through 1950. Not all states allow free access to birth, death, marriage, divorce, and burial records.

Volunteers may enter data incorrectly, especially when attempting to spell names that have been poorly handwritten in the original sources. When the online sources give other spellings of names, those variant spellings are given in this book.

If readers have information that is different from what is provided, please contact the editor and corrections will be made in future editions.

Note: Most of the first-generation individuals are deceased. However, a few are still alive as of this writing. In those cases, minimal information is given to protect their privacy. In some places, the first generation's children, grandchildren, and great-grandchildren names are listed, but no further information is given.

Genealogy

You are about to enter a world that is partly an art, partly a science, and mostly frustration! While you think you are looking for information about the lives and relationships of your ancestors, you are really not prepared for what you may find.

You think you know who your family is (was). Remember, they are humans who lie, cheat, steal, kill, commit adultery, and all sorts of other unsavory things. Then you'll get to the bad folks in your tree! You'll find that other "genealogists" haven't been quite as diligent as they should have been. (Oops, we left lazy out of the above list of sins!)

So how should you tell the story of your lineage? Should you be "prudish," thinking my relatives could never have done that! Oh, yes, they could . . . and did! Should you be "kind" and decide that [someone] doesn't need to know who her father really was?

We need to remember that genealogy is what it is . . . a study and documentation of the lives of people; the good, the bad, and the ugly. Don't we owe it to ourselves and future generations to report it in as accurate a way as possible by telling like it is (was) while remaining sensitive to the feelings of the current generation?

—Paul Andre, Columbia, Missouri

Contents

Introduction 1

Maternal Cook Family 2

Summary of Maternal Sixth Generation and Beyond 2

    George H. Milliken 4

    Agness West Milliken 5

    Jabez Townsend 9

    Mary Bailey Townsend 9

    John Hartsfield IV 11

    Mary "Polly" Riley Hartsfield 13

    Jesse Olive 14

    Monicah Massey Olive 16

Summary of Maternal Fifth Generation 18

    Amos Milliken 18

    Elizabeth "Betsy" Townsend Milliken 18

    John Hartsfield III 20

    Gillie Olive Hartsfield 21

Summary of Maternal Fourth Generation 24

    William Monroe Milliken 24

    Grulia Ann "Gillie" Hartsfield Milliken 29

Summary of Maternal Third Generation 37

    Sarah Elizabeth "Ballie" Milliken Cook 37

Paternal Cook Family 41

Summary of Paternal Fifth Generation 43

    Wesley Cook 41

    Elizabeth Cook 43

    John Joseph O'Brien 43

    Mary O'Brien 44

Summary of Paternal Fourth Generation 44

    Edmund Cook 45

    Mary Ann O'Brien Cook 45

Summary of Paternal Third Generation 56

    Elias Power Cook 56

Summary of Maternal/Paternal Second Generation **61**

    Tera Monroe Cook 61

    Rupert Berber Cook 63

    Heber Amos Cook 67

    Ruby Irma Cook Stover 69

    Eric Power Cook 77

    Gela Lela Cook Moorman 83

Summary of Maternal/Paternal First Generation **113**

    Kenneth Harold Cook 113

    Raymond Berber "R.B." Cook 113

    Ardyce May Cook Banker 113

    Scott Elias Cook 113

    Leota Lucille Cook Pigg 114

    Joseph Doyle Cook 114

    Betty Lavelle Cook Ballmer 114

    Clyde Walter Stover 115

    Ruby Emma Stover Willoughby 115

    Mildred Louise Stover Van Artsdalen 115

    Gela Pearl Stover Stevenson 115

    Mary Elaine Stover Resch 115

    Donald William Cook 115

    Margaret "Peggy" Louise Cook 115

    Virginia Merle Moorman 116

    Enid Eloise Moorman 116

    Eleanor Rose "Mickey" Moorman 116

Introduction

While researching the life of Virginia Merle Moorman, information was discovered about many of her ancestors. This book details the family ancestors of Gela Lela Cook, Virginia's mother. A separate book will provide information about the family ancestors of Oscar Myron Moorman, Virginia's father.

Using online websites and Virginia's notes, details for names, birth and death dates, burial locations, spouses, and children were found. While some of these are names and dates, it is interesting to see where the Cook maternal and paternal families originated and how far they traveled to various places.

It was also interesting to see the number of children born and the span of years in which they were born. On the Cook maternal side (up to the sixth generation), the average number of children that families had was 6, ranging from 1 child to 14 children in the family. The children were born over an average of 14 years, spanning 1 year to 34 years. On the Cook paternal side (up to the sixth generation), the average number of children that families had was 5, ranging from 1 child to 12 children in the family. The children were born over an average of 9 years, spanning 1 to 22 years.

Where known, the cause of death and the age when the person died has been listed. From the 1500s to about 1800, people in Europe lived between 30 and 40 years of age. In the US, life expectancy in the 1860s was about 40 and rose to about 80 in 2020. It dropped during the Civil War (1861-1865), World War 1 (1914-1918), and the Spanish flu epidemic (1918-1920).

The Cook maternal family life expectancy (up to the sixth generation for ancestors over 18) was 68 years for males and 60 years for females, ranging to 96 years for males and 92 years for females. The Cook paternal family life expectancy (up to the sixth generation for ancestors over 18) was 84 years for males and 77 years for females, ranging to 97 years for males and 87 years for females.

Several men from the Cook maternal family served in the US military, including the Revolutionary War, the War of 1812, the Confederate Army in the US Civil War, and the Mexico War. Two sons were from the same family. Several men from the Cook paternal family served in the military, including the Confederate Army in the US Civil War and World War 2.

Color Coding for Maternal Cook Names

The following color coding has been used to help readers trace the generations.

First generation: parents, aunts, uncles
Second generation: grandparents, great-aunts, great-uncles
Third generation: great-grandparents
Fourth generation: great-great-grandparents
Fifth generation
Sixth generation

Virginia Moorman's mother was Gela Lela Cook Moorman.
Gela Moorman's mother was Sarah Elizabeth "Ballie" Milliken Cook.
Ballie Cook's parents were William Monroe and Grulia Ann "Gillie" Hartsfield Milliken.
Monroe Milliken's parents were Amos and Elizabeth "Betsy" Townsend Milliken.
Gillie Milliken's parents were John III and Gillie Olive Hartsfield.
Amos Milliken's parents were George H. and Agness West Milliken.
Betsy Milliken's parents were Jabez and Mary Bailey Townsend.
John Hartsfield III's parents were John IV and Mary "Polly" Riley Hartsfield.
Gillie Hartsfield's parents were Jesse and Monicah Massey Olive.

~~~

Maternal Cook Family

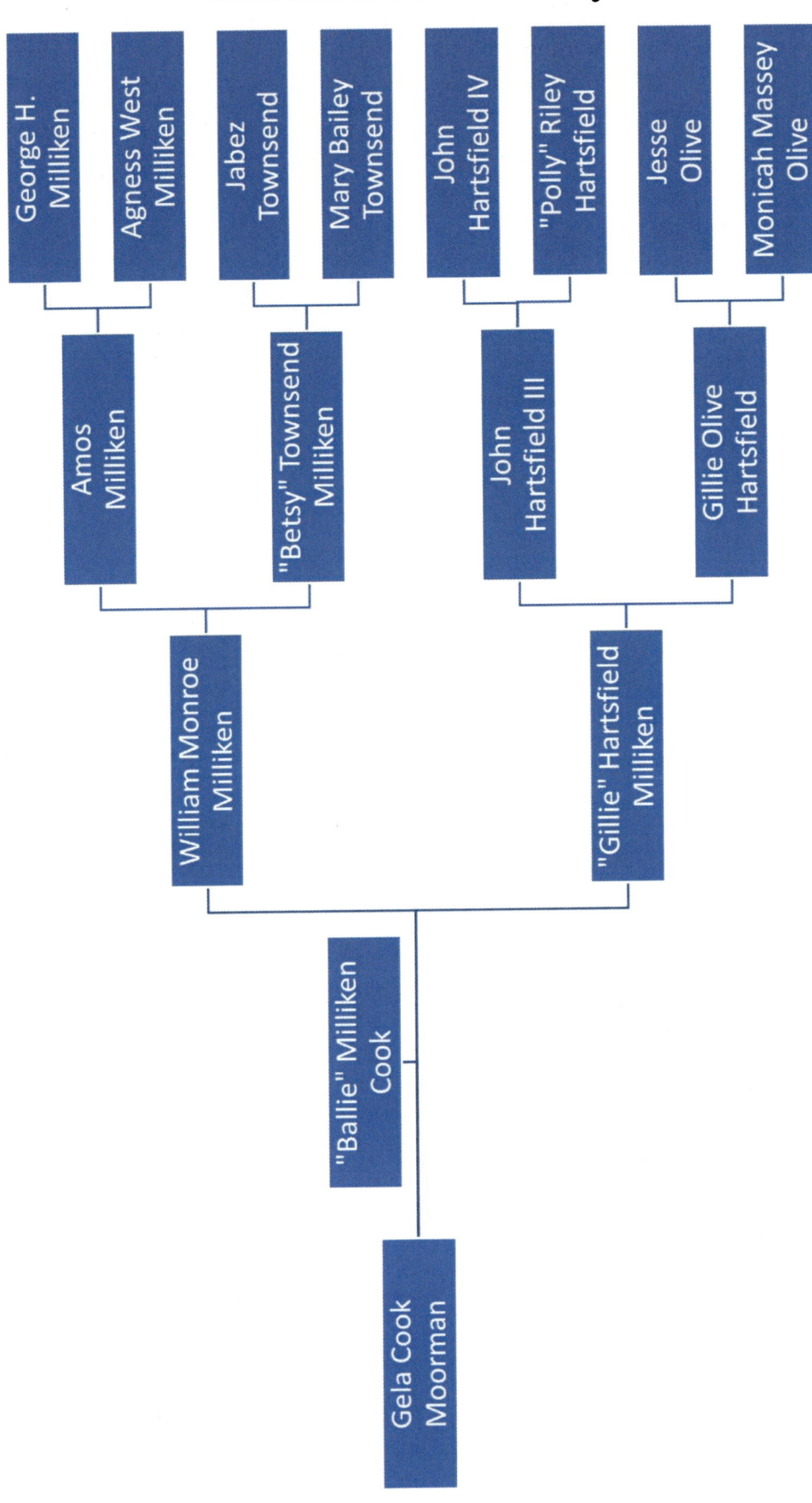

Cook Maternal Family Ancestor Locations

England—Testwood, Yorkshire, Derbyshire, Manchester, Lancashire, Northamptonshire, London, Essex, Surrey, Middlesex, Buckinghamshire, Somerset, Oxfordshire, Hertfordshire, Cumberland, Northumberland, Lincolnshire, Devon, Staffordshire, Sussex, Cheshire, Norfolk, Suffolk, Berkshire: 1481-1653
Virginia—Buncombe, West Point, New River, Hanover, New Kent, Bruton Parish, Green Springs, Jamestown, Elizabeth City, Gloucester, Montross: 1517-1770
Scotland—Ayr, Tranent, Gibson Mill, Edinburgh, Glasgow, Avon: 1570-1670
Germany—Wussingen: 1610-1650
Connecticut—Norwalk, New Haven, Saybrook: 1620-1719
Massachusetts—Boston, Salem, Worcester: 1623-1750
New Jersey—Waterford, Gloucester, Amwellbury: 1652-1713
Pennsylvania: 1665-1750
Maryland: 1717
North Carolina—Hillsborough: 1715-1764
Delaware—Sussex: 1735
Ireland—Connaught: 1736
North Carolina, Guilford County, Greensboro area, 1795: Amos Milliken birth, Gela's maternal great-grandfather (about 80 miles from Raleigh)
Kentucky, Logan County, Russellville area, 1796: Elizabeth "Betsy" Townsend Milliken birth, Gela's maternal great-grandmother
North Carolina, Wake County, 1796: John Hartsfield III birth, Gela's maternal great-grandfather
North Carolina, Wake County, Raleigh area, 1797: Gillie Olive Hartsfield birth, Gela's maternal great-grandmother (about 80 miles from Greensboro)
Kentucky, 1815: Amos Milliken and Betsy Townsend marriage, had two children from 1824 to 1826
North Carolina, Wake County, 1815: John and Gillie Olive Hartsfield marriage, had 8 children from 1816 to 1831
Tennessee, Henry County, Paris area, 1824: William Monroe Milliken birth, Gela's maternal grandfather
1827: John and Gillie Olive Hartsfield moved from North Carolina to Tennessee
Tennessee, Henry County, 1829: Grulia Ann "Gillie" Hartsfield Milliken birth, Gela's grandmother
Tennessee, 1845: Monroe Milliken and Gillie Hartsfield marriage, had 10 children from 1845 to 1869
Tennessee, Henry County, 1856: Amos Milliken death
Tennessee, Paris, 1859: Sarah Elizabeth "Ballie" Milliken Cook birth, Gela's mother
Kentucky, McCracken County, Paducah area, 1875: Betsy Townsend Milliken death
Tennessee, Henry County, 1870: Gillie Hartsfield Milliken death
Tennessee, Henry County, 1876: John Hartsfield III death
Tennessee, Henry County, 1880: Gillie Olive Hartsfield death
Tennessee, Henry County, 1896: William Monroe Milliken death
Missouri, Independence, 1921: Ballie Milliken Cook death, moved in Missouri in 1905 with husband, Elias Power Cook, and children.

Cook maternal family ancestors from Ireland (1736), Scotland (1570), England (1481), and Germany (1610).

Amos Milliken 1795-1824

Hartsfield 1786-1827

Townsend 1796-1875

Monroe and Gillie Milliken 1824-1896

Elias and Ballie Cook moved to Missouri in 1905. Her family remained in Tennessee.

Summary of Maternal Sixth Generation

George H. Milliken traced to 1570 and the 13th generation with European origins in Ireland and Scotland; ancestors were also born in Kentucky, Massachusetts, North Carolina, and Virginia. There is one sir in the Cook family lineage.

Agness West Milliken traced to 1500 and the 14th generation with European origins in England and Scotland; ancestors were also born in Connecticut and Virginia. Titles include sir, major, captain, reverend, and lady.

George (18) and Agness (16) married in Virginia and had 11 children in 28 years.

Amos Milliken is the Cook family ancestor. See details in Maternal Fifth Generation.

~~~

Jabez Townsend traced to 1710 and the 8th generation with origins in Delaware and Virginia.

Mary Bailey Townsend traced to 1712 and the 8th generation with origins in Virginia. Mary's father, Captain John Carroll Bailey, served in the American Revolution, 1778–1781.

Jabez (24) and Mary (16) married in Kentucky and had 3 children in 13 years.

Betsy Townsend Milliken is the Cook family ancestor. See details in Maternal Fifth Generation.

~~~

John Hartsfield IV traced to 1650 and the 9th generation with European origins in Germany; ancestors were also born in Maryland, New Jersey, and Pennsylvania. John served in the US Revolutionary War. He received a land grant of 640 acres in North Carolina, and his wife Mary received a widow's pension after John's death. There is a handwritten copy of his Last Will and Testament.

Mary "Polly" Riley Hartsfield ancestors unknown.

John (39) and Polly (28) married in North Carolina and had 6 children in 13 years.

John Hartsfield III is the Cook family ancestor. See details in Maternal Fifth Generation.

~~~

Jesse Olive traced to 1599 and the 10th generation with European origins in England; ancestors were also born in North Carolina and Virginia. Of note, there is an earl/baron and a lady/countess in the lineage. There is a handwritten copy of his Last Will and Testament.

Monicah Massey Olive traced to 1747 and the 7th generation with origins in Virginia.

Jesse (23) and Monicah (12) married in North Carolina and had 8 children in 13 years.

Gillie Olive Hartsfield is the Cook family ancestor. See details in Maternal Fifth Generation.

~~~

George H. Milliken

Born 1760 (Virginia); died 17 May 1813 at age 53 (Adairville, Kentucky). Unknown burial location. Married Agness West in 1778. Unable to determine what his middle name was—perhaps Harbison?

George H. Milliken Ancestors beyond Sixth Generation

7. George H. Milliken's parents were **Charles Milliken** (born 1736, Connaught, Ireland; died 1785, Chatham, North Carolina) and **Ann Harbison Milliken** (born 1737, Green Springs, Virginia; died 12 May 1785, Spring Hill, Tennessee). Charles and Ann married 6 May 1761 (Stanford, Virginia).

~~~

8. Charles Milliken's father was **Thomas E. Milliken** (born 3 Nov 1693, Ayr, Scotland; died 1778, Chester, Pennsylvania). Mother unknown.

Ann Harbison Milliken's parents were **William Harbison** (born 1706, Virginia; died 12 May 1787, Sullivan, Tennessee) and **Mary (Polly) Harbison** (born 1703; died 1793, Sullivan County, Tennessee). Unknown marriage date. William and Mary's parents unknown.

~~~

9. Thomas E. Milliken's parents were **John Milliken** (born 1664, Boston, Massachusetts; died 1749, Scarborough, Maine) and **Agnis Muire Milliken** (born 1670, Tranent, Scotland; unknown death date). Unknown marriage date.

~~~

10. John Milliken's parents were **Hugh Milliken, Sir** (born 1632, Scotland; died 1668, Boston, Massachusetts) and **Eleanor Allison** (born 1629, Scotland; died 1681, Boston, Massachusetts). Hugh and Eleanor married 1651 (Boston, Massachusetts). Eleanor's parents unknown.

Agnis Muire Milliken's father was **James Muire** (born 1641, Dalkeith, Edinburgh, Scotland; died 1689, New Kent, Virginia) and **Lady Agnes Crichton** (born 1643 Scotland; died 1685, Scotland). Agnes's parents unknown.

~~~

11. Hugh Milliken's parents were **Joseph Knowles Milliken** (born 1600, Gibson Mill, Scotland; died 1650, Boston, Massachusetts) and **Margaret Buchanan** (born 1605, Gibson Mill, Scotland; unknown death date). Unknown marriage date.

James Muire's parents were **George Muire** (born 1620, Edinburgh, Scotland; died Scotland) and **Isabella Miller Muire** (born ~1620, Scotland; died Scotland). George and Isabella married ~1639 (Edinburgh, Scotland). George's parents unknown.

~~~

12. Joseph Knowles Milliken's parents were **Robert Milliken** (born 1570, Glasgow, Scotland; died Boston, Massachusetts) and **Leah Knowless** (born 1575, Scotland; died 1625, Scotland). Unknown marriage date. Robert and Leah's parents unknown.

Margaret Buchanan's parents were **John Buchanan** (born 1580, Scotland; died Augusta County, Virginia) and **Margaret Patton** (born Scotland; died Virginia). Unknown marriage date. John's parents unknown.

Isabella Miller Muire's parents were **Archebald Miller** (unknown birth and death dates) and **Agnes Greir** (born ~1600, Edinburgh Parish, Scotland, unknown death date). Unknown marriage date. Archebald and Agnes's parents unknown.

~~~

13. Margaret Patton's mother was Janet Dagleich (no information). Father unknown.

~~~

Agness West Milliken

Born 26 May 1762 (Green Springs, Virginia); died 6 May 1848 at age 85 (Spring Hill, Tennessee). Buried House Cemetery (Puryear, Tennessee). Married George H. Milliken in 1778. Agness's parents died when she was 8 years old.

Interesting Ancestor of Agness West Milliken

Temperance Flowerdew and George Yeardley, 11th generation, were an important part of the Jamestown Colony (a three-season TV show was created about them). In 2018, Temperance was named one of the Virginia Women in History. Temperance was one of 60 survivors (out of 500) of the "starving" winter of 1609–1610, when Jamestown, Virginia, colonists subsisted on roots, herbs, acorns, berries, and fish. Temperance Flowerdew was named one of the Virginia Women in History by the Library of Virginia in 2018. See https://en.wikipedia.org/wiki/Temperance_Flowerdew.

Temperance married (1) Richard Barrow (1580-1610) on 29 Apr 1609 in London, England. They set sail for Jamestown in June 1609 onboard the *Falcon,* as part of a convoy of nine ships. Temperance arrived in Jamestown in August 1609, while the ship that George Yeardley (her second husband) was on, *Sea Venture,* part of the same convoy, encountered a storm and was shipwrecked on Bermuda. Everyone on the *Sea Venture* survived and arrived at Jamestown in May 1610.

Temperance married (2) George Yeardley (1587-1627) in 1613 (Jamestown, Virginia). George was the deputy governor of Virginia for three years and was knighted in 1618. There is a British television show, *Jamestown* (2017–2019), that depicts the lives of George and Temperance. See below and https://en.wikipedia.org/wiki/George_Yeardley.

Temperance married (3) Francis West (1586-1633) on 31 Mar 1628 (Temperance died Dec 1628). West arrived as part of the second supply of Jamestown settlers in Sep 1608. He served as deputy governor of the colony and also of Virginia. After Temperance died, West fought (unsuccessfully) for possession of her wealthy estate, but it remained with her three children, ages 7, 10, and 12. See https://en.wikipedia.org/wiki/Francis_West.

On July 24, 2018, archaeologists from Jamestown Rediscovery and the Smithsonian Institution announced the discovery of a prominent burial around 400 years old in an important spot within the church. Ground-penetrating radar confirmed the presence of a skeleton of the right age and build for Yeardley who died in 1627 aged about 40.

As of October 2022, it has not been determined if the bones are those of George Yeardley. There are several online resources that provide updates. See Jamestown Rediscovery at https://historicjamestowne.org/archaeology/1617-church/chancel-grave/

Left: Knight's Tombstone, Jamestown, Virginia. Right: Sir George Yeardley, 1587-1627, died age 39.

~~~

Agness West Milliken's Ancestors beyond Sixth Generation

7. Agness's parents were **Robert West** (born 1720, West Point, Virginia; died 1770, Green Springs, Virginia) and **Susanna Isabel Fike** (born 1737, Hanover, Virginia; died 1770, Green Springs, Virginia). Robert and Susanna married 1751 (Virginia).

~~~

8. Robert West's parents were **John West III** (born 1676, West Point, Virginia; died 1734, West Point, Virginia) and **Judith Armistead** (born 1680, Elizabeth City, Virginia; died 1750, West Point, Virginia). John and Judith married 15 Oct 1695 (Elizabeth City, Virginia).

Susanna Isabella Fike's parents were **John Thomas Fike** (born 1719, Norwalk, Connecticut; died 1788, Chatham, North Carolina) and **Elizabeth Sarah Malachi** (born 1715, Virginia; died 1790, Chatham, North Carolina). Unknown marriage date. Elizabeth's parents unknown.

~~~

9. John West III's parents were **John West II** (born 6 Jun 1632, Chicksack Bellfield Plantation, Virginia; died 15 Nov 1689, West Point, Virginia) and **Unity Croshaw** (born 1632, West Point, Virginia; died 20 Apr 1689, New Kent, Virginia). John and Unity married 1667.

Judith Armistead's parents were **Anthony Armistead** (born 1645, Elizabeth City, Virginia; died 26 Oct 1726, Elizabeth City, Virginia) and **Hannah Ellyson** (born 1644, New Kent, Virginia; died 19 Dec 1728, Elizabeth City, Virginia). Anthony and Hannah married 1698 (Elizabeth City, Virginia).

John Thomas Fike's parents **John Fike (Fitch) Jr.** (born 29 Sep 1677, Norwalk, Connecticut; died 5 Apr 1748, New Canaan, Connecticut) and **Lydia Bushnell** (born 1683, Norwalk, Connecticut; died 23 Aug 1786, Clapboard Hill, Connecticut). John and Lydia married 1702 (Danbury, Connecticut).

~~~

10. John West II's parents were **John West, Captain** (born 14 Dec 1590, Testwood, England; died 1 Mar 1659, West Point, Virginia) and **Anne Clairborne Percy** (born 1590, England; died 10 Apr 1667, Williamsburg, Virginia). John and Anne married 1613 (Hants, England). John and Anne's parents unknown.

Unity Croshaw's parents were **Joseph Croshaw, Major** (born 8 Nov 1610, Bruton Parish, Virginia; died 10 Apr 1667, Bruton Parish, Virginia) and **Elizabeth Yeardley** (born 1615, James City, Virginia; died 1666, Bruton Parish, Virginia). Joseph and Elizabeth married 1631 (Virginia).

Anthony Armistead's parents were **William Thompson Armistead** (born 3 Aug 1610, Kirkdeighton, Yorkshire, England; died 13 Jun 1671, Hampton City, Virginia) and **Anne E. Ellis** (born 1 Jul 1611, Yorkshire, England; 4 Dec 1678, Elizabeth City, Virginia). William and Anne married 1632. Anne's parents unknown.

Hannah Ellyson's parents were **Robert Ellyson, Captain** (born 1615, Avon, Scotland; died 28 Sep 1671, Gloucester, Virginia) and **Elizabeth Susannah Gerrard** (born 1627, Lancashire, England; died 17 Sep 1716, St. Marys, Maryland). Robert and Elizabeth married 1643 (Maryland). Robert's parents unknown.

John Fike (Fitch) Jr.'s parents were **John Fike (Fitch) Sr.** (born 10 Jun 1653, Bocking, Essex, England; died 8 Feb 1760, Norwalk, Connecticut) and **Rebecca Lindall** (born 20 Oct 1653, New Haven, Connecticut; died 1704, Norwalk, Connecticut). John and Rebecca married 3 Dec 1674 (Norwalk, Connecticut). John's parents unknown.

Lydia Bushnell's parents were **Francis Bushnell** (born 6 Jan 1649, Saybrook, Connecticut; died 4 Oct 1697, Danbury, Connecticut) and **Hannah Seymour** (born 12 Dec 1654, Norwalk, Connecticut; died Jan 1723, Danbury, Connecticut). Francis and Hannah married 12 Oct 1675 (Norwalk, Connecticut). Francis's parents unknown.

~~~

11. Joseph Croshaw's parents were **Raleigh Croshaw, Captain** (born 4 Dec 1570, Crashaw, Lancashire, England; died 22 Nov 1624, York County, Virginia) and **Ursula Unity Katherine Daniels** (born 1576, Lancashire, England; died Dec 1624, York County, Virginia). Raleigh and Ursula married ~1590 (England) and again in 1603 (York, Virginia). Raleigh Croshaw arrived in Jamestown, Virginia, in Sep 1608 as part of the second supply. Raleigh's and Ursula's parents unknown.

Elizabeth Yeardley's parents were **George Yeardley, Sir** (born 1587, baptized 28 Jul 1588, Southwark, London, England; died 13 Nov 1627, Jamestown, Virginia, buried Third Jamestown Church, Virginia) and **Temperance Flowerdew, Lady** (born 1590, Hethersett, Norfolk, England; died Dec 1628, Jamestown, Virginia).

William Thompson Armistead's parents were **Anthony Armistead** (born 1587, Kirkdeighton, Yorkshire, England; died 15 Nov 1642, Kirkdeighton, England) and **Frances Thompson** (born 28 Jan 1588, Deighton, Yorkshire, England; died 25 June 1634, Deighton, Yorkshire, England). Anthony and Frances married 1608 (Deighton, Yorkshire, England). Anthony and Frances's parents unknown.

Elizabeth Susannah Gerrard's parents were **Thomas Gerrard, Sir** (born 10 Dec 1608, Newhall, Lancashire, England; died 16 Oct 1673, Machodoc, Virginia) and **Susannah Snow** (born 19 April 1609, Staffordshire, England; died 1666, Saint Clement Shores, Maryland). Thomas and Susannah married 21 Sep 1629 (England). Thomas's and Susannah's parents unknown.

Sir Thomas Gerrard, 1608-1673, died age 64.

Rebecca Lindall's parents were **Henry Lindall, Rev.** (born 1632, New Haven, Connecticut; died 29 Sep 1660, New Haven, Connecticut) and **Rozamond Street** (born 1620, New Haven, Connecticut; died 12 May 1682, New Haven Connecticut). Henry and Rozamond married 1650 (Connecticut). Rozamond's parents unknown.

Hannah Seymour's parents were **Thomas Seymour** (born 15 Jul 1632, Norwalk, Connecticut; died 22 Dec 1709, Norwalk, Connecticut) and **Hannah Sarah Marvin** (born 1 Oct 1634, England; died 16 Sep 1712, Connecticut). Thomas and Hannah married 5 Jan 1654 (Connecticut). Thomas's and Hannah's parents unknown.

~~~

12. George Yeardley's parents were **Ralph Yardley** (born 21 Nov 1549, Southwark, Surrey, England; died 25 Oct 1604, Surrey, England) and **Rhoda Marston** (born 17 Jun 1568, Southwark, Surrey, England; died 3 Jan 1603, Southwark, Surrey, England). Ralph and Rhoda married 15 Nov 1575 (Southwark, Surrey, England). Ralph was a London merchant-tailor.

Temperance Flowerdew's parents were **Anthony Flowerdew, Sir** (born 1565, Hetherset, Norfolk, England; died 1610, Hetherset, Norfolk, England) and **Martha Stanley** (born 1570, Norfolk, England; died 2 Dec 1626, Norfolk, England). Unknown marriage date. Martha's parents unknown.

Henry Lindall's father was **Robert Lindall** (born 1600, England; died 8 Sep 1640, St. Bride's Parish, London, England).

~~~

13. Ralph Yardley's parents were **William Edward Yardley** (born 1523, Yardley, England; died 1592, St. James, England) and **Elizabeth Maston Moreton, Lady** (born ~1527, Chester, Cheshire, England; died 7 Jan 1592, St. James, England). William's and Elizabeth's parents unknown.

Rhoda Marston's parents were **James Robert Marston** (born 5 Sep 1548, London, England; died 20 Jun 1599, Surrey, England) and **Catherine Chevall** (born 1544, England; died 11 Apr 1597, London, England). James and Catherine married in about 1560 (England). James's and Catherine's parents unknown.

Anthony Flowerdew's parents were **William Candler Flowerdew** (born 1530, Hethersett, Norfolk, England; died 1600, Scattow, Norfolk, England) and **Frances Appleyard** (born 1530, Scattow, Norfolk, England; died 1600, Scattow, Norfolk, England). William and Frances married 1551 (Livermere, Norfolk, England).

Robert Lindall's father was **William Lindall II** (born 1577, England; died 8 Sep 1640, London, England. William's parents unknown.

~~~

14. William Flowerdew's parents were **John Flowerdew of Hethersett** (born 1500, Hethersett, Norfolk, England; died 16 Dec 1564, Norfolk, England) and **Katherine "Kate" Sheares** (born 1510, Norfolk, England; died 1565, Norfolk, England. John's and Katherine's parents unknown.

Frances Appleyard's mother was **Elizabeth Scott** (born 1504, London, Middlesex, England; died Dec 1549, Norwich, Norfolkshire, England). Father unknown. Elizabeth's parents unknown.

~~~

Summary of George and Agness Milliken Family

George H. Milliken (18) and Agness West (16) married 1778 (Green Springs, Virginia). They had 11 children in 28 years.

1. James Milliken (1781, Chatham County, North Carolina-30 Sep 1836, Shelby County, Illinois) married Mary "Polly" Hastings (1782-1849) on 4 Sep 1805 (Knoxville, Tennessee). They had 10 children: ***Eliza Jane Milliken Williams*** (1807-1835), ***Hanna Milliken*** (1808-1855), ***John Milliken*** (1811-1860), ***Sarah Milliken Williams*** (1814-1860), ***James Milliken*** (1817-1850), ***Samuel Milliken*** (1818-1866), ***Abraham Milliken*** (1820-1845), ***George Milliken*** (1821-1875), ***Jesse (male) B. Milliken*** (1825-1873), ***Abigail Milliken*** (1826-1855). Father James buried Ridge Cemetery, Lakewood, Illinois.

2. William Milliken (Apr 1785, North Carolina-7 Dec 1847, Sulphur Spring, Kentucky) married Mary "Polly" West (1791-1851) on 9 Aug 1808 (Logan, Kentucky). They had 11 children. ***Frances Milliken Harper*** (1809-1841), ***Alfred Milliken, Dr.*** (1811-1840), ***Leonard Hugh Milliken, Rev.*** (1813-1884), ***Agnes Ann Milliken Eddings*** (1819-after 1850), ***William Wesley Milliken*** (1821-1850), ***Leonhard Hiram Milliken*** (1825-1890), ***Mary C. Milliken*** (1827-1855), ***George Wesley Milliken*** (1829-1863), ***Irene Elizabeth Milliken Darby*** (1831-1861), ***Nancy "Nannie" B. Milliken*** (1834-1846), ***Isabella Thompson Milliken Dawson*** (1837-1905).

3. Leonard Hugh Milliken (1793, Guilford, North Carolina-1867, Trinity, Texas) married Mary "Polly" Copeland (1793-1870) on 3 Jan 1816 (Logan, Kentucky). They had 9 children: ***Mahala J. Milliken Wright*** (1816-1835), ***Henry Milliken*** (1816/1818-?), ***George Hugh Milliken*** (1818-1868), ***John Charles Milliken*** (1820-1868), ***Agnes F. Milliken Tucker*** (1824-1870), ***Martha Ann Milliken Ware*** (1825-1862), ***Elizabeth Milliken*** (1829-?), ***Robert Hamilton Milliken*** (1835-1863), ***William R. Milliken*** (1840-after 1861). Some of the family moved to Texas in the 1830s. John Charles Milliken was in the Confederate Army and served as a 2nd lieutenant in the Texas Militia. Robert Hamilton Milliken was in the Confederate Army. He was wounded and had to walk home after the war ended. He died 6 weeks after his return.

4. Amos Milliken (10 Mar 1795, Guilford, North Carolina-21 Nov 1856, Spring Hill, Tennessee). See details in Maternal Fifth Generation.

5. Mary Esten "Polly" Milliken Orndorff (29 Jun 1796, Guilford, North Carolina-17 Jan 1872, Tazewell, Illinois) married Esau Orndorff (1790-1877) in 1815. They had 12 children: ***William Loreign Orndorff*** (1816-1825), ***Benjamin Franklin Orndorff*** (1819-1912), ***Ophelia Orndorff Sherman*** (1821-1899), ***George W. Orndorff*** (1823-1890), ***Mary Ann Orndorff Milner*** (1825-1870), ***Francis Marion Orndorff*** (1827-1852), ***Barbara Jane Orndorff Vaughn*** (1829-1864), ***Noah Orndorff*** (1831-1856), ***Susanah Orndorff Vaughn*** (1833-1911), ***Enoch Thomas Orndorff*** (1835-1920), ***Van Orndorff*** (1839-1902), ***Levi Orndorff*** (1844-1900). On 12 Oct 1860, George W. Orendorff's wife and two daughters were murdered when a man tried to rob them at home. Mary buried in Orendorff Cemetery (Hopedale, Tazewell County, Illinois).

6. Spencer Milliken (1799, North Carolina-1812, Logan, Kentucky). Died age 14.

7. George Milliken (1804, Logan, Kentucky-1843, Red River, Texas) married Sarah Martin (1815-1870). They moved from Kentucky to Texas in 1839. In the 1850 US Census, Sarah has moved back to Henry County, Tennessee, after George died in 1843. They had 7 children: ***Thomas Evermont Milliken*** (1830-1830, died 8 months old), ***John Charles Milliken*** (1832-1882), ***Elizabeth Agnes Milliken*** (1834-1901), ***Sarah Milliken Jr.*** (1837-after 1850), ***George Amos Milliken*** (1840-1861, died age 21), ***Nancy Ann Milliken Poyner*** (1842-1910), ***Pamela Ann Milliken*** (before 1843-before 1850, died age 7).

8. Elizabeth Milliken (1806, Logan, Kentucky-Aug 1839, Henry, Tennessee). Died age 33.

9. Nancy H. Milliken Crewdson Young (1808, Logan, Kentucky-Aug 1839, Henry, Tennessee) married (1) Samuel Bell Crewdson (1802-1833) in Apr 1825 (Kentucky). They had 4 children: ***William Newman Crewdson, Captain*** (1826-1903), ***James W. "J. W." Crewdson, Rev.*** (1828-1896), ***John M. Crewdson*** (1830-1833, died age 3), ***Samuel Bell Crewdson, Captain*** (1833-1864). After Samuel's death, Nancy married (2) James Young (1797-1850) in 1837 (Tennessee). They had 1 child: ***Andrew W. Young*** (1838-1863, died in the Battle of Chancellorsville, Virginia, US Civil War). William Crewdson served in the Mexico War (1846-1848). Son Samuel was listed as a brick mason in the 1860 US Census. He later died in the US Civil War. Son Andrew also died in the US Civil War.

10. Agness Milliken (1809, Logan, Kentucky-1839, Henry, Tennessee). Died age 30.

Three sisters, Elizabeth, Nancy, and Agness, died in 1839 in Henry County, Tennessee.

~~~

Amos Milliken is the Cook family ancestor. See details in Maternal Fifth Generation.

~~~

Jabez Townsend

Born 15 Jun 1762 (Orange County, North Carolina); died 1 Nov 1817 at age 55 (Logan County, Kentucky). Buried Jabez Townsend Cemetery (Anderson, Logan County, Kentucky). Married Mary Bailey (1770-1847) 11 Sep 1786 (Kentucky).

Jabez Townsend's Ancestors beyond Sixth Generation

7. Jabez Townsend's parents were **Thomas Townsend Sr.** (born 1735, Delaware; died 20 May 1796, South Carolina) and **Anaphileda Watson Townsend** (born 1730, Hanover County, Virginia; died Dec 1818, Logan County, Kentucky). Thomas and Anaphileda married ~1758 (Orange County, North Carolina). Thomas Townsend was in the Revolutionary War.

~~~

8. Thomas Townsend Sr.'s parents were **Benedictus Townsend** (born 1710; died 1769) and **Lucilla Light Townsend** (born 1715; died 1769). Benedictus and Lucilla's parents unknown.

Anaphileda Watson Townsend's parents were **John T. Watson** (born 4 Mar 1710, Hanover Virginia; died 1 Feb 1760, Henrico, Virginia) and **Euphemia Alice Grisell Townsend** (born 1710, Hanover, Virginia; died 1794, Chatham, Pittsylvania, Virginia). John and Euphemia's parents unknown.

~~~

Mary Bailey Townsend

Born 1770 (Henry County, Virginia); died 1847 at age 77 (Harlan County, Kentucky). Buried Jabez Townsend Cemetery (Anderson, Kentucky). Married Jabez Townsend 11 Sep 1786 (Kentucky).

Mary Bailey Townsend's Ancestors beyond Sixth Generation

7. Mary Bailey Townsend's parents were **John Carroll Bailey, Captain** (born 4 May 1748, Northumberland, Virginia; died 3 Jul 1816, Lincoln, Kentucky) and **Priscilla Townsend** (born 1751; died 22 Jun 1810). Unknown marriage date. Priscilla's parents unknown.

"John Bailey joined General George Rogers Clark's Expedition to the Old Northwest Territory in 1778. After Clark's toilsome and hazardous march of 240 miles from Kaskaskia, Ill., Bailey, then a Lieutenant, was sent in advance with a detachment of men to begin the attack and fire on Fort Sackville, at Vincennes, Indiana, on the Wabash River, occupied by a force of British and Indians. The surprise attack began about 8:00 o'clock on the night of February 23, 1779. Lieutenant Bailey led the center of the successful attack, and his party was the first to arrive within firing distance of the fort. He was with General Clark from the beginning of the Campaign, and 'was in all the leading expeditions, and a faithful and efficient officer everywhere.' He was made a Captain in March 1780, was in command at Fr. Jefferson that year, and in Command at Vincennes until November 1781."
—The Kentucky Society of the Sons of the American Revolution, 13 May 1943

~~~

8. John Carroll Bailey's parents were **George Bailey** (born 11 Jan 1712) and **Ann Bradley** (no information). George and Ann's parents unknown.

~~~

Summary of Jabez and Mary Townsend Family

Jabez Townsend (24) and Mary Bailey Townsend (16) married 11 Sep 1786 (Kentucky). They had 3 children in 13 years.

1. William Townsend (3 Mar 1794, Logan County, Kentucky-13 Jul 1875, Cassville, Missouri) married (1) Mary Langston (1798-1842) on 18 Aug 1814 (Kentucky). They had 11 children: **Winford Green Townsend** (1815-1890), **Nancy Jane Townsend** (1817-1863), **Jabez Ragland Townsend** (1820-1867), **Allen Molecion Townsend** (1822-1907), **Malissa Ann "Lizzie" Townsend Britt** (1824-1884), **Thomas Bailey Townsend** (1826-1908), **Lilueeta Ann "Lucetta" Townsend Barnes** (1827-1883), **Drucilla Dicena "Diccie" Townsend Kelly** (1827-1912), **Mary Cordelia Townsend** (1828-1888), **William Mangrum Alexander Townsend** (1832-1889), **Bryant Mervin Townsend** (1837-1909).

After Mary died, William married (2) Emily Lane (1804-after 1860) on 20 Oct 1842 (Greene County, Missouri). They had 2 children: **James Robert Townsend** (1847-1848), **Jefferson Bailey Townsend** (1843-1917).

William's history is documented in *Opening the Ozarks: First Families of Southwest Missouri, 1835-1839*, by Marsha Hoffman Rising, published in 2005 by American Society of Genealogists.

2. Elizabeth "Betsy" Townsend Milliken (11 Mar 1796-17 Jan 1875). See details in Maternal Fifth Generation.

3. Allen Townsend (7 Dec 1807, Kentucky-2 Jan 1897, Texas) married (1) Susan S. Ross (1810-1855) in 1832. She is listed as his wife in the 1850 US Census. They had 11 children: **Davis Townsend** (1835-after 1850), **Sarah Townsend** (1836-1906), **Lucinda Townsend** (1837-after 1850), **Alzada Townsend** (1838-after 1850), **Thomas Townsend** (1840-after 1850), **James L. Townsend** (1844-after 1860), **William A. Townsend** (~1843-after 1860), **Susan Elizabeth "Lizzie" Townsend Sears** (1844-1936), **Louisa Holmes Townsend** (1846-1930), **Matilda Townsend** (1849-after 1860), **H. J. Townsend** (~1853-after 1860).

After Susan died, Allen married (2) Martha Hester Ann Carpenter Cawthorn (1827-before 1870) on 23 Jan 1856 (Clark, Arkansas). Martha had 4 children: **Saby B. Cawthorn** (~1838-after 1860), **Rehuhema Cawthorn** (~1849-after 1860), **Adolphus J. Cawthorn** (~1853-after 1860), **Larkin Cawthorn** (~1856-after 1860). They had 3 children: **Martha Frances Townsend Smith** (1859-1924), **Roda Ella Townsend** (1861-1934), **Charles Townsend** (1869-?).

Allen later married (3) Elizabeth S. Estell Poer (1829-1901). She is listed as his wife in the 1870 US Census. Elizabeth had 3 children: **Cynthia Jane Poer Darr** (1851-1872), **Frances Marion Poer** (1854-after 1943), **John Milton Poer** (1863-1944). Allen is listed as a widower, living with one daughter, in the 1880 US Census.

Jabez and Mary Townsend's sons. Left: William Townsend, Oak Hill Cemetery, Cassville, Missouri, died age 81.
Right: Allen Townsend, Rough Creek Cemetery, Granbury, Texas, died age 89.

~~~

Betsy Townsend Milliken is the Cook family ancestor. See details in Maternal Fifth Generation.

~~~

John Hartsfield IV

Born 4 Sep 1751 (Johnston County, North Carolina); died 27 Apr 1821 at age 69 (Wake County, North Carolina). Unknown burial location. Married Mary "Polly" Riley Hartsfield (1762-1854) on 22 Feb 1790 (Wake County, North Carolina). John's father died when he was 8 years old and his mother died when he was 10 years old.

John served in the US Revolutionary War (1775-1781), North Carolina Cavalry, as a private under Captain Lewis Bledsoe. For service in the Revolutionary War, the federal government granted John Hartsfield IV 640 acres in Wake County, North Carolina, land grant 739, issued 28 Oct 1782, location "on both sides of Harry Swipes Creek." Mary received a widow pension of $33.87 per year. John had a last will and testament.

In the **1790 US Census,** John lived in Wake County, North Carolina, listing 1 white male over the age of 16, 2 white females, and 1 slave.

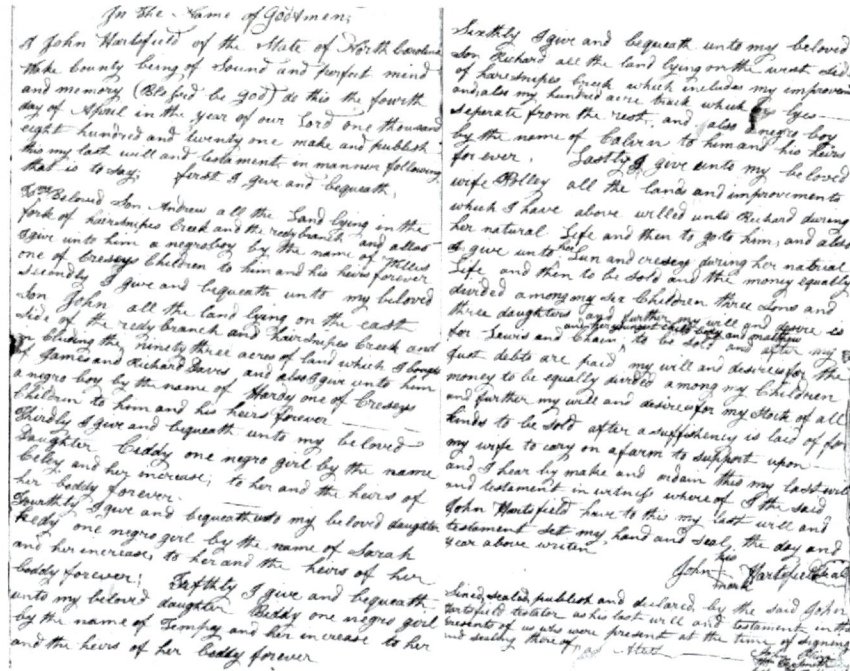

Last Will and Testament of John Hartsfield IV, 4 April 1821.

In the Name of God Amen;

"I John Hartsfield of the State of North Carolina Wake County being of Sound and perfect mind and memory (Blessed be God) do this the fourth day of April in the year of our Lord one thousand eight hundred and twenty one make and publish this my last will and testament, in manner following that is to say; first I give and bequeath,

To my Beloved Son Andrew all the Land lying in the fork of hairsnipes [Harry Swipes] Creek and the redy brank and also I give unto him a negro boy by the name of Willis one of Creseys Children to him and his heirs forever

Secondly I give and bequeath unto my beloved Son John all the land lying on the east Side of the Redy branch and the hairsnipes Creek and including the ninety three acres of land which I bought of James and Richard Davis and also I give unto him a negro boy by the name of Hardy one of Creseys Children to him and his heirs forever

Thirdly I give and bequeath unto my beloved Daughter Ciddy one negro girl by the name of Celey and her increase; to her and the heirs of her boddy forever.

Fourthly I give and bequeath unto my beloved daughter Kedy one negro girl by the name of Sarah and her increase, to her and the heirs of her boddy forever;

Fifthly I give and bequeath unto my beloved daughter Biddy one negro girl by the name of Tempy and her increase to her and the heirs of her boddy forever

Sixthly I give and bequeath unto my beloved Son Richard all the land lying on the west side of haresnipes Creek which includes my improvements and, also my hundred acre track which lyes seperate from the rest, and also a negro boy by the name of Calvin to him and his heirs forever.

Lastly I give unto my beloved wife Polley all the lands and improvements which I have above willed unto Richard during her natural Life and then to go to him, and also I give unto her Lun and Cresey during her natural Life and then to be sold and the money equally divided among my six children three sons and three daughters and further my will and desire is for Lewis and Chain and her youngest child bedy and matthew to be sold and after my just debts are paid my will and desire is for the money to be equally divided among my Children and further my will and desire is for my Stock of all kinds to be sold after a sufishency is laid of for my wife to cary on a farm to support upon and I hear by make and ordain this my last will and testament in witness where of I the said John Hartsfield have to this my last will and testament set my hand and seal the day and year above writen.

[his mark] John Hartsfield

Sined, sealed, publish and declared, by the said John Hartsfield testator as his last will and testament in the presents of us who were present at the time of signing and sealing there of, attest

John Olive
Wm F. Smith
[his mark] Joshua Todd"

John Hartsfield IV's Ancestors beyond Sixth Generation

7. John Hartsfield IV's parents were **Andrew John Hartsfield** (born 3 Jan 1713, Philadelphia, Pennsylvania; died 11 Nov 1761, Wake County, North Carolina) and **Sara Lynn Burck/Burk** (born 1715, Baltimore County, Maryland; died Mar 1759, Johnston County, North Carolina). Andrew and Sara married 1734 (Baltimore County, Maryland). Sara's parents unknown.

~~~

8. Andrew Hartsfield's parents were **Godfrey Hartsfield** (born 1685, Germantown, Philadelphia, Pennsylvania; died 1745, Craven County, North Carolina) and **Katherine Walter** (born 1690, Waterford, New Jersey; died 14 Oct 1717, North Carolina). Godfrey and Katherine married 1710 (Waterford, New Jersey). Katherine's parents unknown.

~~~

9. Godfrey Hartsfield's parents were **Jurian Georgius Hartsvelder** (born 1650/1654, Wussingen, Germany; died 1 Jan 1690, Chester, Philadelphia, Pennsylvania) and **Margaret Pawling** (born 1665, Germantown, Philadelphia, Pennsylvania; died 21 Aug 1732, Germantown, Pennsylvania). Jurian arrived in the US in 1676. Jurian and Margaret married 25 Mar 1678 (Philadelphia, Pennsylvania). Jurian's and Margaret's parents unknown.

~~~

Mary "Polly" Riley Hartsfield

Born 1762 (Wake County, North Carolina); died Dec 1854 at age 92 (Wake County, North Carolina). Unknown burial location. Married John Hartsfield IV on 22 Feb 1790 (Wake County, North Carolina). Mary's parents unknown.

~~~

Summary of John and Polly Hartsfield Family

John Hartsfield IV (39) and Mary "Polly" Riley Hartsfield (28) married 22 Feb 1790 (Wake County, North Carolina). They had 6 children in 13 years.

1. **Andrew "Rew" Hartsfield III** (7 Feb 1792, Wake County, North Carolina-23 Aug 1856, Spring Ridge, Louisiana) married Ghasky Hartsfield (1797-1849) on 24 Jul 1817 (Oglethorpe County, Georgia). They had 8 children: **Mary Hartsfield** (1820-1820), **James R. Hartsfield** (1820-1864), **John Riley Hartsfield** (1822-1874), **Elizabeth Amanda Hartsfield** (1829-1869), **Sarah C. "Sallie" Hartsfield Shadowen** (1831-1900), **Rev. Green Washington Hartsfield** (1831-1900), **Andrew Sidney Hartsfield** (1834-1864), **William Jasper Hartsfield** (1839-1897).

2. **John Hartsfield III** (22 Jun 1794, Wake County, North Carolina-13 May 1876, Henry County, Tennessee). See details in Maternal Fifth Generation.

3. **Cynthia "Siddy" Hartsfield Blake** (29 Dec 1796, Wake County, North Carolina-19 Feb 1880, Gibson, Tennessee) married Asa Blake (1795-1850) on 26 Jan 1814 (Wake County, North Carolina). They had 3 children: **Dempsey A. Blake** (1828-1901), **John S. Blake** (1831-1880), **Williamson A. Blake** (1836-1877).

4. **Katherine Kezeah "Kitty" Hartsfield Hill** (1798, Wake County, North Carolina-Aug 1856, Wake County, North Carolina) married Wiley Hill (1790-1834) on 20 Dec 1814 (Wake County, North Carolina). They had 9 children: **Mary Hill** (1815-1856), **John Henry Hill** (1817-1865), **Bethany Hill** (1819-1847), **Biddie Hill** (1821-1843), **Ciddy Emeline Hill** (1821-1915), **Andrew Green Hill** (1822-1907), **William Lorenzo Dow Hill** (1827-1892), **Elizabeth Hill** (1828-1843), **Wiley Ausher Hill** (1831-1920).

5. **Obedience "Biddie" Hartsfield Johns** (4 Oct 1801, Wake County, North Carolina-17 Oct 1875, Winnsboro, Texas) married Jesse Burton Johns (1794-1879) on 29 Nov 1819 (Wake County, North Carolina). They had 4 children: **John Bunyan Johns** (1822-1871), **Sarah DuPriest Johns Ingram** (1825-1882), **William Hartsfield Johns** (1828-1891), **James H. Johns** (1831-1865).

6. **Richard Hartsfield** (6 Jun 1805, Wake County, North Carolina-26 Jul 1891, Brazil, Tennessee) married Penelope "Penny" Simmons (1806-1901) on 11 Apr 1826 (Wake County, North Carolina). They had 11 children: **R. H. Hartsfield** (1827-1850), **Redden S. Hartsfield** (1827-1866), **John Carroll Hartsfield** (1829-1876), **Wiley G. Hartsfield** (1830-1849), **James "Jim" Hartsfield** (1834-1923), **William Sidney Hartsfield** (1834-1923), **Unnamed Male Hartsfield** (1835-1850), **Sara Francis "Fanny" Hartsfield Dinwittey/Denwiddie** (1836-1914), **Mary W. Hartsfield Ragan-Toms** (1838-1880), **Octavia W. Hartsfield Fitzgerald** (1842-1902), **Elizabeth "Betsy" Hartsfield Mitchell** (1844-after 1900).

~~~

John and Polly Hartsfield's grandson Rev. Green Washington Hartsfield, 1831-1900, died age 69.

**John and Polly Hartsfield's daughters. Left: Siddy Blake, Hartsfield Cemetery, Tennessee, died age 83.
Middle: Biddie Johns, Lee Cemetery, Winnsboro, Texas, died age 74.
Right: John and Polly Hartsfield's son Richard Hartsfield, Gibson, Tennessee, died age 86.**

~~~

John Hartsfield III is the Cook family ancestor. See details in Maternal Fifth Generation.

~~~

Jesse Olive

Born 1762 (Johnston County, North Carolina); died 14 Apr 1829 at age 67 (Raleigh, North Carolina). Unknown burial location. Married Monicah Massey in 1782 (Wake County, North Carolina).

"DIED, In this county, on Tuesday morning last, Mr. Jesse Olive, aged about 70."
—*The Star, and North Carolina State Gazette* (Raleigh, North Carolina), Thursday, April 16, 1829.

Last Will and Testament of Jesse Olive, 13 October 1828.

"In the Name of God Amen

I Jesse Olive Senr of the County of Wake and State of North Carolina Being of Sound mind and perfect memmory (Blessed be God) but weak in boddy by health do this the Thirteenth day of October in the year of our Lord one Thousand Eight Hundred and Twenty Eight make and publish this my last will and Testament in the manner following that is to say

First I lend to my Beloved wife Monica Olive my Land plantation Dwelling house and all my out houses during her widowhood Bounded as follows begining at a beach on the bank of Crabtree Creek at the ford leading to the publick mill thence a south course along the old lane to a large persimmon tree thence a south east course so as to take in the spring thence a south course, so as to take in the apple orchard to

14

the south line thence west along said line to a pine Jones' corner thence a south course to a post oak thence west along the heirs of Lanes line to a post oak then a north course to a post oak James Olives & Wm. Nichols' corner then a north east course to a red oak then a north course to Crabtree creek thence down the various courses of said creek to the begining and I also lend to her during her widowhood a negro woman by the name of Anica and a negro boy by the name of Abram & also one bed and furniture a half dozen chairs one pot and Duch oven all the knives & forks & all the earthen ware and her choice of Desk or side board and one Chest her choice; and her choice of the horses & two sows and all their shoats which use about the house and also two of her choice of the cows & calfs and a suffishent quantity of the working tools to carry on her farm and also the Still & cooks, one flax & cotton wheel & one loom & all the water vessels & one walnut folding table & one pine table.

Secondly I give unto my beloved son Richard Olive one negro man by the name of Jerry to him & his wife during there natural life and at there deaths to be sold and equally divided between there children.

Thirdly I give unto my beloved daughter Salley Bowden one negro girl by the name of Lucy

Fourthly I give unto my beloved Son John Olive one negro man by the name of Jacob to him & his wife during there natural life and at their Deaths to be sold and Equally divided between their children.

Fifthly I give unto my beloved Son James Olive all my Land lying on the west side of that which I willed to my beloved wife, and I also give unto him & his wife a negro boy by the name of Abram at the Death of my beloved wife & if she should marry it is my will for my son James then to have him, During there natural life and at there Deaths to be sold and Equally divided between there children.

Sixthly I give unto my beloved Daughter Rachel Smith and her husband one negro woman by the name of Cherry and all her present & future Increase During there natural life and at there Deaths to be Equally divided between there children.

Seventhly I give unto my beloved Daughter Gilley Hartsfield & her husband one negro girl by the name of Fanney & her increase during there natural life and at there Deaths to be Equally divided between there children

Eightly and further my will and desire is that my Executor after my Death Sell or divide all the ballance of the tract of land on which I live on the east side of the land I willed to my beloved wife and also half the tract of land on wich Richard Massey Senr Decd lived and also the tract on which William Lyon now lives and the ballance of the house & furniture and Stock of all kinds gun boat & car and oxen the ballance of the plantation working tools to be sold and that my Executors out of the money arising from the sale of said property after paying all my just debts my will and desire is for them to purchace two negro girls about the sise of them I gave to Salley Rachel & Gilley one for my beloved Daughter Elizabeth Crowder & the other for my beloved Daughter Polley Lyons and that my Executors make them a right in the same manner in which I left the negros to the rest of my children and that the ballance of the money be Equally Divided between my five daughters Salley Rachel Gilley Elizabeth & Polley

Ninthly I give unto my beloved son Jesse Olive all the land and plantation & houses which I have left to my beloved wife at the expiration of her right and further my will and desire is for my son Jesse to live with my beloved wife during her life or widowhood that is if they can agree if not they must divide the plantation; and I also give unto him a negro boy by the name of Reddick to him and his lawfull heirs forever also one plow & weding hoe one half Dozen chairs one set of knives & forks

and further my will and desire is after the Death of my beloved wife that all the property which I have left to her Except the land and negro boy Abram to be sold & the money to be Equally divided between my five Daughters Salley Bowden Rachel Smith Gilley Hartsfield Elizabeth Crowder & Polley Lyon and I hereby make and ordain my worthy friends William F. Smith & Dempsey Bowden my Executors of this my last will & Testament in witness where of I the said Jesse Olive have to this my last will & Testament set my hand and seal the day and year above writen.

[his mark] Jesse Olive

Signed sealed & published and declared by the said Jesse Olive the testator as his last will & Testament in the presents of us who ware present at the time of Signing and Sealing there of

Burwell T. Jones Junior
Berry D. Simms
Jn. B. Johns Junior"

Jesse Olive's Ancestors beyond Sixth Generation

7. Jesse Olive's parents were **James Olive** (born 13 Oct 1713, Gloucester, Virginia; died 22 Jan 1805, Wake County, North Carolina) and **Elizabeth Southwood Grey** (born 15 Oct 1715, Hillsborough, North Carolina; died ~1814 (Wake County, North Carolina). James and Elizabeth married 4 Nov 1735 (Abingdon Parish, Virginia).

~~~

8. James Olive's parents were **William Olive** (born before 1696, England; died 1727, Gloucester, Virginia) and **Mary** (no information). Unknown marriage date. William and Mary's parents unknown.

Elizabeth Southwood Grey's parents were **Thomas Grey** (born 1650, Northumberland, England; died 1730, Guilford, North Carolina) and **Rebecca Booth** (born 1660, England; died 1735, Guilford, North Carolina). Unknown marriage date. Thomas's parents unknown.

~~~

9. Rebecca Booth's parents were **William Booth** (born 1630, England; died 1680, Virginia) and **Lady Elizabeth Grey** (born 1622, Stamford, Lincolnshire, England; died 4 Jan 1690, Burke, Georgia, British America). Unknown marriage date. William's parents unknown.

~~~

10. Elizabeth Grey's parents were **Henry, 1st Earl of Stamford, Second Baron Grey of Groby** (born 1599, Stamford, Northumberland, England; died 21 Jul 1673, Groby Castle, Bradgate, Leicestershire, England) and **Elizabeth, Lady, Countess of Berkshire Cecil** (born 1603, Exeter, Devon, England; died 1 Jun 1680, Newtown, Queens, New York). Henry and Elizabeth married 19 Jul 1620 (Groby, St. Bennet Sherehog, London, England). Henry and Elizabeth's parents unknown.

~~~

Monicah Massey Olive

Born 3 Mar 1773 (Wake County, North Carolina); died 16 Oct 1854 at age 81 (Paris, Tennessee). Buried Hartsfield Cemetery (Paris, Tennessee). Monicah's mother died in 1774, when Monicah was one year old. It appears that Monicah's father remarried and had a daughter (Nancy Levinia Massey Privett) in 1780 with a second wife (no information). Monicah married Jesse Olive ~1785 (Wake County, North Carolina) when she was 12 years old. She probably had her first child at the age of 13.

Monicah Massey Olive, 1773-1854, died age 81.

Monicah Massey's Ancestors beyond Sixth Generation

7. Monicah Massey's parents were **Richard Andrew Massey Sr.** (born 1747, Brunswick County, Virginia; died 23 Mar 1807, Wake County, North Carolina) and **Judith Dorothy Brassfield** (born 1747, Brunswick County, Virginia; died 1774, North Carolina). Richard and Dorothy married about 1767 (North Carolina). Richard and Dorothy's parents unknown.

~~~

Summary of Jesse and Monicah Olive Family

Jesse Olive (23) and Monicah Massey Olive (12) married 1782 (North Carolina). They had 8 children in 13 years.

1. James D. Olive (9 Jun 1784, Wake County, North Carolina-18 Jun 1829, Lauderdale, Alabama) married Sarah "Sally" Hartsfield (1787-1878) on 16 Apr 1812 (Wake County, North Carolina). They had 7 children: **Robert Andrew Olive** (1816-1853), **Archibald Olive** (1818-1903), **William Billum Olive** (1822-1900), **Sarah Gillie Olive** (1824-1865), **James H. Olive** (1826-1860), **Richard Olive** (1827-1896), **Rachel Ann Olive** (1830-1868). James was a War of 1812 veteran: "Seventh Company, Wake County Regiment, NC."

2. Richard J. Calvin Olive (12 Oct 1786, Wake County, North Carolina-10 Apr 1873, Berry, Alabama) married Sarah Mann Drake (1782-1858) in 1810 (North Carolina. They had 10 children: **Patsy Olive** (1810-?), **Elizabeth Drake Olive** (1811-1886), **Martha Matilda Olive Blakney** (1815-after 1880), **Penny Olive** (1817-?), **Richard Calvin Jones Olive** (1817-1895), **Dicy Olive Poe** (1818-after 1880), **Rebecca Olive Roberts** (1820-after 1880), **Andrew Jackson Olive** (1822-1880), **Jesse Olive** (1836-after 1860), **Edward Drake Olive** (1838-1907).

3. Mary "Polly" Olive Lyon (1788, North Carolina-18 Jun 1821, Henry County, Tennessee) married William Washington Lyon (1796-1854) on 18 Jun 1821 (Wake County, North Carolina). Polly died on her wedding day.

4. Sarah "Salley" Olive Bowden (1790, Wake County, North Carolina-1850, Henry County, Tennessee) married Dempsey Bowden (1789-1868) on 19 Dec 1808 (Wake County, North Carolina). They had 11 children: **Penelope Bowden Todd** (1809-1858), **Thomas M. Bowden** (1810-1848), **Grizzie Ann Bowden Crowder** (1812-1879), **Elias Bowden** (1814-1874), **Robert Dempsey Bowden** (1820-1888), **Balder "Baldy" Douglas "B. D." Bowden** (1820-1890), **John H. Bowden** (1820-1880), **Edward Gaynue Bowden** (1825-1888), **Mary Ann Bowden Todd** (1829-1872), **Isaiah H. Bowden** (1831-1899), **Adaline Cornelia Bowden** (1838-1920). Robert and Balder were twins. Dempsey Bowden married Rhoda Owens (1805-1880) in 1850.

5. Elizabeth Olive (1790, North Carolina-1828, Henry County, Tennessee). Died age 38.

6. John Olive (1792, Wake County, North Carolina-1859, Henry County, Tennessee) married (1) Holland Bowden (1797-1842) on 29 Sep 1812 (Wake County, North Carolina). They had 5 children: **Ashley A. Olive** (1818-1910), **Joy Catherine "Icy" Olive Waggener** (1822-1879), **John Henry Olive** (1824-1905), **Rebecca Angeline Olive Stevenson** (1829-1900), **Leonidas Taylor Olive** (1831-1883). Ashley and Rebecca married siblings. After Holland died, John married (2) her sister Mary Bowden (1794-1877) in 1842.

7. Rachael Olive Smith (10 Jul 1796, Wake County, North Carolina-1 Jun 1876, Wake County, North Carolina) married William Fletcher Smith (1791-1856) on 25 Dec 1813 (Wake County, North Carolina. They had 9 children: **Hilliard J. Smith** (1816-1882), **Sarah Smith Cope** (1818-1885), **Elizabeth Smith Phillips** (1819-after 1878), **James Thomas Smith** (1820-after 1880), **William Asbury Smith** (1822-1860), **Wesley Owen Smith** (1824-1863), **Grizzy Ann Smith** (1826-1902), **Nancy Grant Smith Matthews** (1829-1861), **Mary Lueasor Louise Smith Cope** (1832-1864). In the 1870 US Census, mother Rachael lived with her son Hilliard and his wife and their four children, along with her daughter Grizzy Ann on her property in Wake County, North Carolina. In the 1850 US Census, Hilliard was the "overseer" for his sister's farm in Alabama. Elizabeth Phillips lived in Alabama with her 5 children, ages newborn to 7 years old. In 1863, Hilliard married his brother William's wife after he died in 1860.

8. Gillie Olive Hartsfield (1797, Wake County, North Carolina-1880, Henry County, Tennessee). See details in Maternal Fifth Generation.

~~~

Left: Jesse and Monicah Olive's son. Richard J. C. Olive, Tabernacle Cemetery, Berry, Alabama, died age 86. Right: Jesse and Monicah's grandson Ashley A. Olive and spouse Margaret. Unknown date.

~~~

Gillie Olive Hartsfield is the Cook family ancestor. See details in Maternal Fifth Generation.

~~~

Summary of Maternal Fifth Generation

Amos Milliken was born in North Carolina. In 1810, at the age of 15, he was living in Stewart, Tennessee. By 1813, he was living in Kentucky. When he was 20, he married Betsy Townsend in Kentucky. He was 28 when his first son (William Monroe) was born and 31 when his second son (George Melton) was born, both in Tennessee. When he was 55, he was living in Tennessee and his occupation was listed as a farmer. He died at age 61 in Tennessee and is buried at House Cemetery in Henry County, Tennessee.

Betsy Milliken was born in Kentucky. She was 19 when she married Amos Milliken in Kentucky. Research indicates that she had her first child at the age of 27, 9 years after being married. Her second son was born when Betsy was age 30. She died at age 79 in Tennessee. Her burial place is not known.

William Monroe Milliken is the direct ancestor of the Cook maternal family line. See details in Maternal Fourth Generation.

~~~

John Hartsfield III was born in North Carolina. When he was 21, he married Gillie Olive in North Carolina. He and Gillie had their first child when he was 22 and their last child when he was 37. They had 8 children in 15 years. Her was appointed as US Postmaster of McGowan, Tennessee, in 1835. He died at age 81 and is buried in Hartsfield Cemetery in Paris, Tennessee.

Gillie Hartsfield was born in North Carolina. When she was 18 she married John Hartsfield. She had her first daughter when she was 19 and her last daughter when she was 34. She died at age 83 and is buried in Hartsfield Cemetery in Paris, Tennessee.

Grulia Ann "Gillie" Hartsfield Milliken is the direct ancestor of the Cook maternal family line. See details in Maternal Fourth Generation.

~~~

Amos Milliken

Born 10 Mar 1795 (Guilford County, North Carolina); died 21 Nov 1856 at age 61 (Henry County, Tennessee). Buried House Cemetery (Puryear, Henry County, Tennessee). Married Betsy Townsend 25 Jul 1815 (McCracken County, Kentucky). His father died in 1813, when Amos was 18 years old.

~~~

Elizabeth "Betsy" Townsend Milliken

Born 11 Mar 1796 (Logan County, Kentucky); died 17 Jan 1876 at age 79 (Spring Hill, Henry County, Tennessee). Unknown burial location. Married Amos Milliken 25 Jul 1815 (McCracken County, Kentucky).

~~~

Summary of Amos and Betsy Milliken Family

Amos (20) married Elizabeth (19) 25 Jul 1815 (Kentucky). They had 2 children in two years.

1. **William Monroe Milliken** (5 Feb 1824-2 Aug 1896). See details in Maternal Fourth Generation.

2. **George Melton Milliken** (15 Jun 1826, Tennessee-27 Dec 1874, Marshall County, Kentucky). Buried New Harmony Cemetery (Iola, Kentucky). Married Elvira Caba Powell (1830-1874) on 8 Jan 1849 (Henry County, Tennessee). They had 9 children: **Susan Virginia "Jennie" Milliken Bigger** (1849-1875, "died of a child fever after giving birth to Edward Bigger Jr., at the age of 26 years"), **John Bailey Townsend/B.T.** (1852-1929), **Martha/Marietta/Mary E. Milliken Wood** (1854-1884), **Amos W. Milliken** (1857-1914), **Sis/Ella Milliken Phillips Radford** (1861-1942), **Minnie L. Milliken English** (1865-1942), **Nellie Lee Milliken Wallace** (1868-1928), **Lillian Milliken Molin** (1871-1960), **William W. Milliken** (1872-1963).

~~~

In the **1820 US Census,** Amos Milligan [*sic*] is listed as living in Stewart, Tennessee. It's not clear if there is a wife or children listed.

In the **1830 US Census,** Amos Millisan [sic] is listed as living in Henry County, Tennessee. There is one male "under five years of age" (George); one male "of five and under ten" (William); one male "of thirty and under forty" (Amos); one female "of thirty and under forty" (Betsy).

In the **1840 US Census,** Amos Milligen [sic] is listed as living in Henry County, Tennessee. There is one male "5 & under 10" (unknown name); three males "10 & under 15" (George and two unknown names); one male "15 & under 30" (William); one male "40 & under 50" (Amos); one female "40 & under 50" (Betsy); one female "70 & under 80" (probably Betsy's mother, Mary Bailey Townsend).

1850 US Census

Amos (55) and Elizabeth (54) were living with their son George (22) and wife Elvira (20) and their 7-month-old daughter Susan. Listed below is Amos and Elizabeth's other son Wm. Monroe (25) and wife Gilly (20) with their children: Thomas (5), Martha (3), and W. A. (1).

1860 US Census

Amos died in 1856. Elizabeth Milligan [sic] (64) is living with her son George M. (34) and wife Elvira (29) and their children: Susan V. (10), John B. (8), Martha (6), Amos (3), and Sis (2 mo.). Also with the family is Nancy J. Erwin. Note that Elizabeth's in-laws John and Gily [sic] Hartsfield live next door. (Amos and Betsy's son Monroe married John and Gillie's daughter Gillie. Later on this same page, John and Gillie's son S. B. and Malinda Hartsfield live nearby with their children (not shown).

1870 US Census

Geo. M. Milican [sic] (45, mill operator) and Eloyad [Elvira]. Mother Iissabela [Elizabeth] (75). Virginia (20), Bailey (18), Mary E. (16), Amos (13), Elah [Ella] (9), Minie (4), Nellie (2). The Millikens lived next door to John and Sarah Fletcher. Their daughter, Anna Laura (born 1869), married Oscar Amos Milliken (1869-1935), the son of William (George's brother).

George's wife Elvira died 8 Jul 1874 at age 47 of "bilious fever." George died 27 Dec 1874 at age 48 of "pneumonia fever." Their children would have been ages 2 to 25 years old. They're both buried in New Harmony Cemetery in Iola, Kentucky. It's unclear where Betsy went to live after their deaths. It might be that she moved back to Tennessee to live with Monroe, as that's where she died in 1876.

~~~

Amos and Betsy Milliken's son, George Milliken, New Harmony Cemetery, Iola, Kentucky, died age 48.

~~~

William Monroe Milliken is the Cook family ancestor. See details in Maternal Fourth Generation.

~~~

John Hartsfield III

Born 22 Jun 1794 (Wake County, North Carolina); died 13 May 1876 at age 81 (Henry County, Tennessee). Buried Hartsfield Cemetery (Paris, Tennessee). Married Gillie Olive 27 Nov 1815 (Wake County, North Carolina).

John was sworn in as postmaster of the McGowan, Tennessee post office on 1835-04-05.

The role of postmaster was a political appointment. Most were appointed by the General Postmaster with the help of the local congressmen and the recommendation of the community. Appointments for the largest post offices were chosen by the President of the United States with the support of the Senate.

To qualify, John had to be a legal adult and in almost all causes a U.S. citizen. Party affiliations or other relationships could often be drawn between a recently elected politician and a newly appointed postmaster.

The local post office served many roles for the community and postmasters, like John, were often a trusted pillar of the community. They were responsible for overseeing the day to day operations of the post office, timely delivery of the mail, and selling postage.

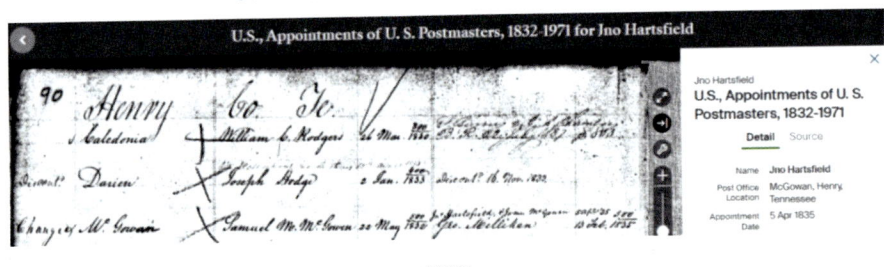

~~~

Gillie Olive Hartsfield

Born 1797 (Wake County, North Carolina); died 1880 at age 83 (Henry County, Tennessee). Gillie was living with her son Simeon and his family in 1880. Buried Hartsfield Cemetery (Paris, Tennessee). Married John Hartsfield III 27 Nov 1815 (Wake County, North Carolina).

Left: John Hartsfield III, Hartsfield Cemetery, Paris, Tennessee, died age 81.
Right: Gillie Olive Hartsfield, Hartsfield Cemetery, Paris, Tennessee, died age 83.

~~~

Summary of John and Gillie Hartsfield Family

John (21) and Gillie (18) married 27 Nov 1815 (North Carolina). They lived in Wake County, North Carolina, until about 1827, then moved to Henry County, Tennessee. They had 8 children in 15 years.

1. **Elizabeth "Eliza" Hartsfield Collier** (22 Nov 1816, North Carolina-5 Feb 1859, Tennessee). Buried in Hartsfield Cemetery (Paris, Tennessee). Married Harvey Withe Collier (~1814-1863) about 1835. They had 5 children: *Erasmus Dudley Collier* (1836-1901), *Mary H. Collier* (1843-after 1850), *Zachary Taylor Collier* (1849-1906), *A. Noel (male) Collier* (1853-after 1900), *E.F. (female) Collier* (1858-11 Feb 1859). After Eliza died, Harvey married Frances Woodson Rowlett (1830-1908) in 1859. They had 1 child: Wilhelmina "Minnie" Cornelia Collier (1860-1927).

2. **Simeon/Sim B. Hartsfield** (17 Nov 1820, Wake County, North Carolina-1 Mar 1891, Tennessee). Buried in Hartsfield Cemetery (Paris, Tennessee). Married (1) Catherine Malinda Crawford (1824-1866) on 21 Dec 1841 (Henry County, Tennessee). They had 11 children: *Bradford Hartsfield* (1843-after 1860), *Elizabeth A. Hartsfield* (1844-after 1860), *Malissa J. Hartsfield* (1846-1871), *Sophia* (1847-after 1860), *M.G./Martha Gilly Hartsfield* (1850-1870), *William B. Hartsfield* (1852-1880), *John W. Hartsfield* (1854-1882), *Nancy Kezia Hartsfield* (1856-after 1870), *Julian D. Hartsfield* (1859-1871), *S. R. "Sudie" Aycock Hartsfield* (1862-after 1880), *Simeon/S.O. Hartsfield* (1864-1885). After Catherine died, Sim married (2) Elizabeth Cloar Crawford (1832-1910) on 25 Nov 1866 (Henry County, Tennessee). Mary had been married to William L. Crawford (1822-1861) and had 5 children. When Simeon and Elizabeth got married, her children (3 boys and 2 girls) would have been ages 5 to 13. Sim and Elizabeth together had 3 children: *Robert Luther Hartsfield* (1868-1951), *Albert Phelps/A.P. Hartsfield* (1873-1966), *Charles/Charlie Harris Hartsfield* (1875-1964). In the **1870 US Census,** S.B. is listed with his wife E. and 11 children living at home, ages 1 to 24. Simeon had 14 children, along with 5 stepchildren, with his two wives in 34 years.

3. **Juliana A. Hartsfield Anderson** (17 Jan 1823, North Carolina-21 Jan 1901, Tennessee). Buried in Hartsfield Cemetery (Paris, Tennessee). Married Richard Anderson (1825-after 1880) on 6 May 1840 (Henry County, Tennessee). They had 1 child: *John P. Anderson* (1844-1855).

4. **G. M. Hartsfield** (17 Sep 1824, North Carolina-4 Oct 1866, Tennessee). Buried in Hartsfield Cemetery (Paris, Tennessee). Died age 42.

5. **Martha Helon Hartsfield Edmonds** (1825, Wake County, North Carolina-28 Aug 1854, Henry County, Tennessee). Buried in Hartsfield Cemetery (Paris, Tennessee). Married Preston Brown Edmonds (1818-1894) on 17 Sep 1840 (Henry County, Tennessee). They had 2 children: **Elizabeth Ann "Bettie" Edmonds Dumas** (1850-1880) and **Cyrus Walker Edmonds** (1853-1907). After Martha died, Preston married Angeline B. Crowder (1833-1894) in 1855. They had 9 children.

6. **John O. Hartsfield** (1827, Wake County, North Carolina-~1890, Hopkins County, Texas). Unknown burial location. Married Martha A. Elizabeth "Mattie" Simmons (1827-1886) on 23 Nov 1849 (Lauderdale County, Alabama). They had 6 children: **Mary Elizabeth Thornton "Mollie" Hartsfield Barclay** (1851-1940), **John Henry Hartsfield** (1852-1899), **Lucretia "Lessy" Hartsfield** (~1853-after 1870), **Simeon "Sim" Hartsfield** (~1855-after 1870), **Georgia Ann Hartsfield Hargrave** (1857-1934), **B. O. Hartsfield** (1860-1866).

7. **Grulia Ann "Gillie" Hartsfield Milliken** (Aug 1829, Henry County, Tennessee-21 Nov 1870, Henry County, Tennessee). See details in Maternal Fourth Generation.

8. **Crotilda/Frotilla Flotilla J. Hartsfield Bates** (1831, Tennessee-4 Aug 1877, Kansas City, Kansas). Buried in Oak Grove Cemetery (Kansas City, Kansas). Married Dr. Ewing Porter Bates (1821-after 1880) on 25 Oct 1852 (Henry County, Tennessee). They had 6 children: **S. W. Bates** (after 1853-1860), **T. R. Bates** (after 1853-1866), **John L. Bates** (1854-1854, 7 mo.), **Charles H. Bates** (~1867-after 1880), **Lula K. Bates Isler** (1870-1930), **Robert A. Bates** (1871-after 1900). Dr. Bates married after 1877 to Mary H. (1827-after 1880).

~~~

In **1835**, John Hartsfield and George Milliken were appointed as US Postmasters of McGowan, Henry County, Tennessee. There is no current town called McGowan in Tennessee. McGowan Branch is a stream about 2 miles from Paris, Tennessee. There were also many family members named McGowan in the area.

In the **1840 US Census**, John Hartsfield is listed as living in Henry County, Tennessee. There is one male "10 & under 15"; one male "15 & under 20"; one male "50 & under 60" (John); one female "5 and under 10"; one female "10 & under 15"; one female "15 and under 20"; one female "40 and under 50" (Gillie).

In the **1850 US Census**, John Hartsfield, age 56, is listed as a "farmer," living in Henry County, Tennessee, with Gilly Hartsfield, age 51, along with their daughter, Crotilda Hartsfield, age 19, and John T. Anderson, age 6 (probably their grandson from Juliana Hartsfield Anderson).

In the **1860 US Census**, John Hartsfield, age 65, is listed as a "farmer," living in Henry County, Tennessee, with "Gila" Hartsfield, age 61. They are living near George Milliken (their daughter Gillie married George's brother Monroe) and their son S. B. Hartsfield and their families.

In the **1870 US Census**, F Hartsfield, age 76, is listed as a "farmer," living in Henry County, Tennessee, with G. Hartsfield, age 74, and W. Milliken, age 21, a "farmer." W. Milliken is probably their grandson, William Alexander "Alex" Milliken, born 1849 to Monroe and Gillie Milliken. They are living near J. Hartsfield (male), age 48, along with 4 children; A. Milliken and family, and S. B. Hartsfield and family.

John died in 1876. In the **1880 US Census**, on 9 June, "Gilla Hartsfield," age 81, is listed as "parilized" and living in Henry County, Tennessee, with her son Simeon Hartsfield, age 59, a "farmer," and his family. The family includes his wife "keeping house"; a son, 26, who "works on farm"; a daughter, 18, "at home"; four sons, ages 4 to 15, "at school"; a stepson (Green Crawford), 20 "works on farm"; a grandchild, 15, "at home" who has "fits" and labeled in the "Idiotic" column. Gillie died 27 Nov 1880.

~~~

JACKSON, Tenn., March 22.—(Special.) E. D. Collier, aged 60, ex-Deputy United States Marshal at McKenzie, is dead. He was one of the best known deputies in this part of the State.

John and Gillie Hartsfield's grandson Erasmus Dudley Collier, Mount Olivet Cemetery, McKenzie, Tennessee, died age 64. Erasmus was a US deputy marshal.

John and Gillie Hartsfield's grandson Zachary Taylor Collier, Mount Olivet Cemetery, McKenzie, Tennessee, died age 57. Pictured with spouse, Ada Medora Harris Collier, 1854-1939.

John and Gillie Hartsfield's children. Left to right: Simeon Hartsfield, Hartsfield Cemetery, Paris, Tennessee, died age 70; G.M. Hartsfield, Hartsfield Cemetery, Paris, Tennessee, died age 42; Elizabeth Collier, Hartsfield Cemetery, Paris, Tennessee, died age 42; Martha Edmonds, Hartsfield Cemetery, Paris, Tennessee, died age 29.

Left: John and Gillie Hartsfield's son, John O. Hartsfield, died age 63. Middle: John and Gillie Hartsfield's grandson John Henry Hartsfield with spouse Jennie Shanklin and 3 of 6 children. Right: John Henry Hartsfield, Sulphur Springs City Cemetery, Sulphur Springs, Texas, died age 46.

> DIED.—In this city, on Friday, August 4th, at 10 o'clock, a. m., Mrs. F. J. Bates, wife of Dr. E. P. Bates. She died in the full triumph of christian faith and many times during her long and painful sickness she exhorted her husband and children to live so as to meet her in Heaven.   B.

> **DIED.**
>
> BATES– In Wyandotte City, Kansas, on the fourth day of August, 1877, Mrs. F. J. BATES, wife of Dr. E. P. Bates, for many years residents of Memphis.

John and Gillie Hartsfield's daughter, Mrs. F. J. Bates, died age 46.

~~~

Gillie Milliken is the Cook family ancestor. See details in Maternal Fourth Generation.

~~~

Summary of Maternal Fourth Generation

William Monroe Milliken was born in Tennessee. He went by Monroe. He was 20 when he married Gillie Hartsfield in Tennessee. He had his first child when he was 21. He had his last child with Gillie when he was 45. Gillie died in 1870 and Monroe married Sarah in 1872, adding her two sons to the family. Monroe and Sarah had one daughter in 1880.

Monroe died at age 72 in Tennessee and is buried in Milliken Cemetery in Henry County, Tennessee. There are several documents from the Tennessee Wills and Probate Records that show an inventory of Monroe's belongings, sale of items, distribution of assets, and an arbitration decision.

Grulia Ann Hartsfield was born in Tennessee. She was known as Gillie. She married Monroe when she was 16. They had 10 children in 24 years. Gillie died in 1870, at age 41, one year after her last child was born. She left 8 children, ages 2 to 23, with Monroe, age 46. Two daughters died the next year, in 1871, and Monroe married again in 1872.

Monroe and Gillie's children died at ages 7 months to 72 years. Two children preceded Gillie in death: Her oldest son, Tom, died in 1869 at age 24, and her youngest son, George, died in August 1870 at 7 months. Monroe outlived five of his children with Gillie. In addition to Tom and George, three of his daughters preceded him in death: Martha died in 1881 at age 34, Josie died in 1871 at age 20, and Nannie died in 1871 at age 18.

There were also a variety of causes of death including mitral regurgitation (Alex), died suddenly (Jennie), pneumonia (Charlie), brain tumor (Ballie), and cancer (Amos).

Sarah Elizabeth "Ballie" Milliken Cook is the direct ancestor of the Cook maternal family line. See details in Maternal Third Generation.

~~~

William Monroe Milliken

Born 5 Feb 1824 (Henry County, Tennessee); died 2 Aug 1896 at age 72 (Henry County, Tennessee). Buried in Milliken Cemetery (Henry County, Tennessee). Married (1) Grulia Ann "Gillie" Hartsfield Milliken on 2 Jan 1845 (Henry County, Tennessee). Monroe and Gillie had 10 children in 24 years.

After Gillie's death, he married (2) Sarah J. Farmer Cox Milliken (1834-1886) on 28 Jan 1872 (Henry County, Tennessee). Sarah had two sons from her previous "Cox" marriage: Gova (born ~1856) and John (born ~1860). Monroe (56) and Sarah (46) had 1 daughter, Bertie Monroe "Roe" Milliken Clark (1880-1914). Sarah died in 1886 when Roe was 6 years old. It's likely that all the older children were gone from the home by that time. It doesn't appear that Monroe remarried, and it's unclear who might have helped to care for Roe.

W. Monroe Milliken, 1824-1896, died age 72.

The following images are from the State of Tennessee, Henry County, Wills and Probate Records for W.M. Milliken, who died without a will. His son-in-law E. P. Cook (married to Ballie Milliken, Monroe's daughter) was administrator for the estate.

Administrator's Bond, 12 Dec 1896.

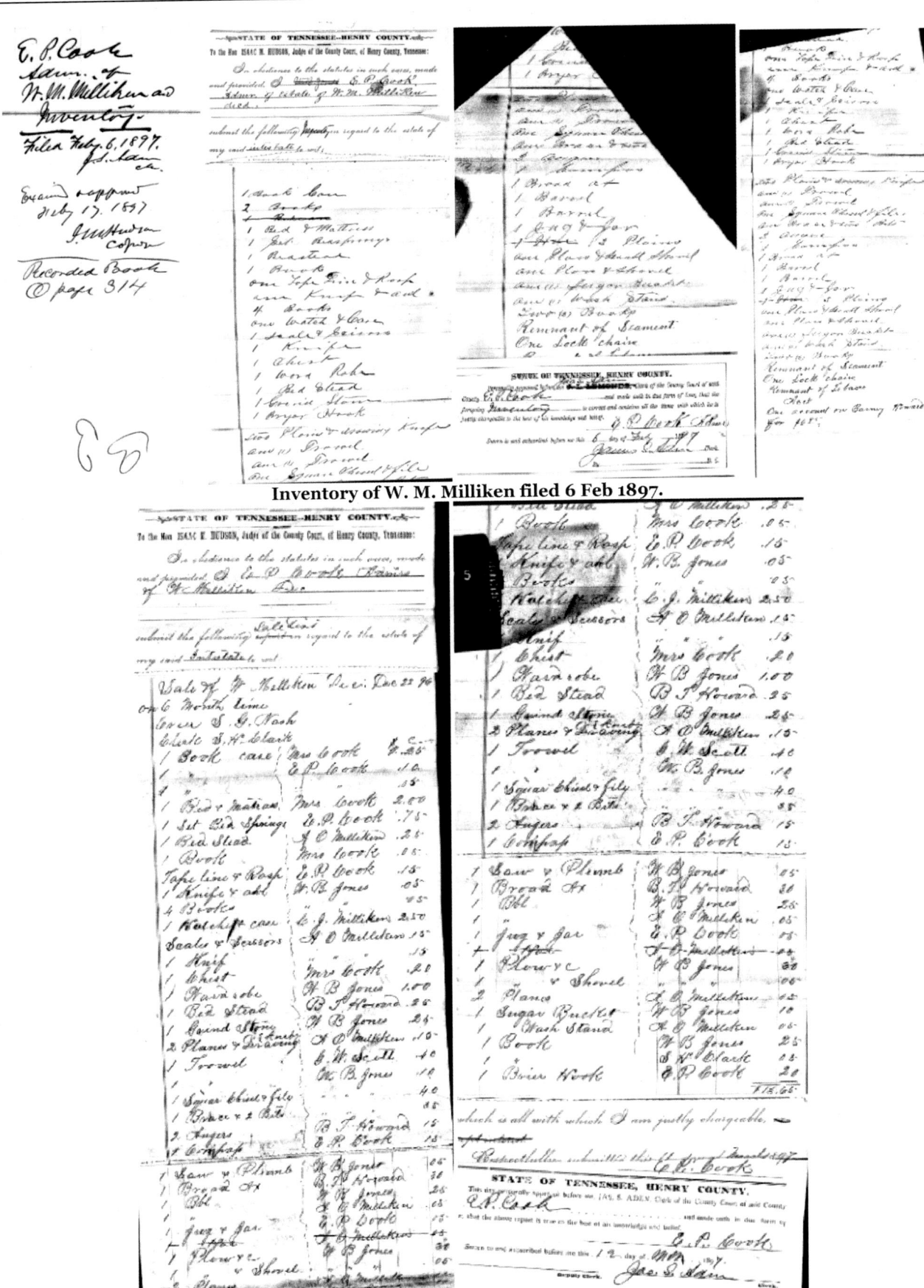

Inventory of W. M. Milliken filed 6 Feb 1897.

Sale list of $13.65 for items sold belonging to W. M. Milliken estate, starting 22 Dec 1896 and reported on 12 Mar 1897.

Left: image shows title page of Reports & Settlement, dated 1 Dec 1899.
Right: image shows receipt of $275.55 for sale of items, land, and interest, 30 Nov 1899.

Image shows total of $289.20 for sale list. After settling debts and paying $20 to the administrator, there was a balance for distribution of $72.43 to seven heirs of Monroe Milliken. His children (Jennie Hays, Alex Milliken, Charlie Milliken, Ballie Cook, Ossie Milliken, Roe Clark) received $10.33. His grandchild (Eddie Todd) received $10.35.

Arbitration decision between Osie Milliken and E.P. Cook. 9 Feb 1897.

"Where as we the undersigned Osie Milliken and E. P. Cook are parties to an arbitration in which Osie Milliken is son & heir at law of the late W. M. Milliken deceased & in which the said Osie Milliken claimes that the said W. M. Milliken had before his death given him to have and to hold as his own certain property to wit. One Bureau & one mule & he also claims that he is ~~ought~~ not ~~for~~ liable for rents from his majority till deceaseds death

and in which E. P. Cook as admin. of the estate of the above named W. M. Milliken claimes that the evidence in reguard to the above named property, and rents is not sufficiesh to warrant him as admin. against the lawful claimes of any and all heirs & creditors of the said W. M. Milliken and having been advised by County Judge of Henry County Tenn. as to the legality of the following procedure.

Now there fore know all men by these present that we the undersigned Osie Milliken and E. P. Cook have agreed to select each a man ~~& they to select a third man~~ to act as arbitrators in the aboved named case& after having heard the evidence on both sides to decide what is wright in the premises and J. L. Steward and Alexander Wilson ~~and they having selected~~ having been selected ~~as the third man~~ we bind our selves each to other upon our word and honor to abide by & perform the decision of the arbitrators in the case.

Feb 9th 1897

E. P. Cook Admrs
A. O. Milliken"

"We the undersigned having been selected as arbitrators to decide a controvercy between Osie Milliken is son and heir at law of the late W. M Milliken and in which E. P. Cook is Admin of the estate of the late W. M. Milliken deceased

After having heard the evidence on both side have decided that the above name Osie Milliken is entitled to the property & rent in controvercy to wit one bureau one mule & the rent on the hands of the late W. M. Milliken up to & inclusive of the year 1896.

Feb 9th 1897

J. L. Stewart
Alex Wilson"

~~~

Grulia Ann "Gillie" Hartsfield Milliken

Born Aug 1829 (Henry County, Tennessee); died 21 Nov 1870 at age 41 (Henry County, Tennessee). Buried in Hartsfield Cemetery (Paris, Tennessee). Married William Monroe Milliken 2 Jan 1845 (Henry County, Tennessee).

Grulia Ann "Gillie" Hartsfield Milliken, 1829-1870, died age 41.

~~~

Summary of Monroe and Gillie Milliken Family

Monroe (21) married Gillie (16) on 2 Jan 1845 (Tennessee). They had 10 children (all born in Henry County, Tennessee) in 24 years.

1. Alonzo Thomas Milliken (6 Dec 1845, Henry County, Tennessee-1869, Henry County, Tennessee). Known as Thomas. Died age 24.

2. Martha Helen Milliken (30 Aug 1847, Henry County, Tennessee-Jan 1881). Died age 34.

3. William Alexander "W.A./Alex" Milliken (15 Mar 1849, Henry County, Tennessee-28 Oct 1917, Eaton, Tennessee). Died age 68 of "mitral regurgitation of heart." Buried Old Mayfield Cemetery (Eaton, Tennessee). Married Alabama E. "Bammie" Crowder (1847-1919) in 1879 (Tennessee). Bammie's death certificate lists the cause of death as "Pellagra," a severe vitamin B3/niacin deficiency. They had 2 children: **Sula Eve Milliken Childress** (1879-1903), **Thomas Milliken** (1886-1955).

4. Amanda Josephine "Josie" Milliken (1 Apr 1851, Henry County, Tennessee-17 Dec 1871, Henry County, Tennessee). Buried Hartsfield Cemetery (Paris, Tennessee). Died age 20, 16 days after her sister.

5. Nancy Edna "Nannie" Milliken (14 Jun 1853, Henry County, Tennessee-1 Dec 1871, Henry County, Tennessee). Buried Hartsfield Cemetery (Paris, Tennessee). Died age 18, 16 days before her sister.

6. Eugenia "Jennie" Porter Milliken Shell Hays (27 May 1855, Henry County, Tennessee-3 Apr 1920, Cottage Grove, Tennessee). Died age 65 "suddenly." Buried Hays Cemetery (Cottage Grove, Tennessee). Married (1) Perry Frank "P.F." Shell (1848-after 1880) 17 Aug 1873 (Henry County, Tennessee). They had 3 children: **Bernard Shell** (1875-after 1880), **Ethel Nancy Shell Cloys** (1877-1944), **Seba S. Shell** (1880-1953). The 1880 US Census lists Shell as a farmer, cannot read or write, living in Saint Francis, Clay County, Arkansas, with "Jenie" and extended family.

Jennie married (2) Samuel A. "S. A." Hays (1856-1913) in 1884 (Tennessee). They had 7 children: **Ross R. Hays** (1884-1901), **Minnie May Hays Olive** (1887-1960), **Mary A. "Munsey" Hays** (1889-1906), **Curtis Maxwell "Buck" Hays** (1891-1961), **Alma Lee Hays McVay Wallace** (1894-1989), **Ballie Hays** (1896-1908), **Naoma Hays** (1899-1925). The 1900 US Census lists Hays as a farmer, living in Henry County, Tennessee, with Jennie and 3 children.

7. Charles John Milliken (29 Jul 1857, Henry County, Tennessee-10 Oct 1929, Benton County, Tennessee). Died age 72 of "T. B. pneumonia broncal and paralis." Buried in Birds Creek Cemetery (Whitlock, Tennessee). Married Martha Agnes Crawford Milliken (1857-1941) in 1882 (Henry County, Tennessee). They had 3 children: **Herman Highbank Milliken** (1883-1948), **Josephine Eva Milliken Puryear** (1885-1956), **Holmes Crawford Milliken** (1888-1966).

8. Sarah Elizabeth "Ballie/Sallie Beth" Milliken (7 Oct 1859, Henry County, Tennessee-5 Oct 1921, Independence, Missouri). See details in Maternal Third Generation.

9. Amos Oscar "A.O./Ossie" Milliken (16 Jul 1868, Henry County, Tennessee-27 Oct 1935, McCracken County, Kentucky). Died age 67 of "carcinoma of stomach." Buried Wallace Cemetery #1 (Iola, Kentucky). Married Anna [Annie] Laura Fletcher (1869-1894) on 6 May 1888. They had 2 children: **Guy W. Milliken** (1889-1912), **Ina Pearl Milliken Wallace** (1891-1941). Anna died at age 24; Guy was 5 and Pearl was 3. Guy and Pearl were friends with Gela Cook and wrote her postcards (see "Postcards to Gela Cook" later in this book for examples). Oscar Milliken married Mary R. Ward Martin (1882-1966) after 1910. Mary was widowed and had 1 child from a previous marriage: **Ruth E. Martin Lindsey** (1906-1985). Oscar and Mary had 1 child: **Roy Monroe Milliken** (1915-2002).

10. George Simeon Milliken (16 Dec 1869, Henry County, Tennessee-2 Aug 1870). Died age 7 months. Buried Hartsfield Cemetery, Paris, Tennessee.

11. Bertie Monroe "Roe" Milliken (3 Aug 1880, Tennessee-2 Dec 1914, Whitlock, Tennessee). Died age 34. Buried Oak Hill Union Church Cemetery (Osage, Tennessee). Married Robert Armstead Clark (1864-1929) on 20 Aug 1899.

~~~

Monroe and Gillie Milliken's son. Left: William Alexander Milliken, Old Mayfield Cemetery, Eaton, Tennessee, died age 68. Right: spouse Alabama E. "Bammie" Milliken, died ag3 72.

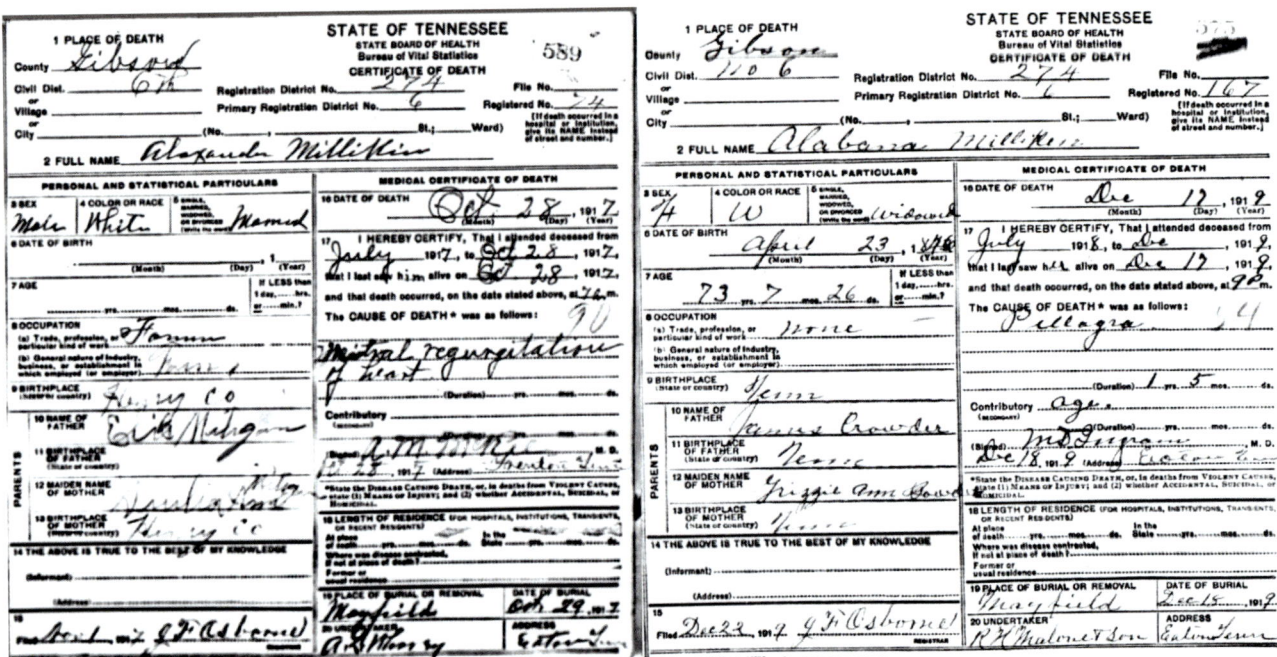

Alexander and Alabama Milliken's death certificates.

30

Monroe and Gillie Milliken's grandson Tom Milliken, Oakwood Cemetery, Dyer, Tennessee, died age 69.

Monroe and Gillie Milliken's daughters. Left and middle: Amanda Josephine "Josie" died age 20. Right: Nancy Edna "Nannie" died age 18. Both buried Hartsfield Cemetery, Paris, Tennessee.

MRS. JENNIE MILLIKEN HAYS CALLED TO BEYOND

Mrs. Jennie Milliken Hays, age 66 years, died suddenly at her home near Cottage Grove, last Friday. She was a much beloved woman, high in principle, and careful of the beautiful little things that make life so worth living.

At the age of eighteen she was married to Mr. P. E. Shell, to which union three children were born, two of whom survive her, Mrs. W. H. Cloys of Paris, Tenn., and Mr. Seba Shell of Oakland, California.

In 1884 she was married to Mr. Samuel A. Hays, who preceded her to the grave seven years.

To this union seven children were born, four of whm survive her, Mrs. J. W. Olive, Mrs. H. W. McVey, Miss Naoma Hays and Mr. Curtis M. Hays.

She also leaves one sister, Mrs. Ballie Cook of Independence, Mo., and two brothers, Mr. Charlie Milliken of Cottage Grove, Tenn., and Mr. Ossie Milliken of Paducah, Ky., to mourn her loss.

In early life she united with the Missionary Baptist church, exemplifying the life of a true Christian to the end.

The Parisian, Paris, TN, Friday, April 9, 1920

Monroe and Gillie Milliken's daughter, Eugenia "Jennie" Porter Milliken Shell Hays, Hays Cemetery, Cottage Grove, Tennessee, died age 64.

Monroe and Gillie Milliken's grandchildren, children of Jennie and Samuel Hays

Left: Ross R. Hays, Hays Cemetery, Cottage Grove, Tennessee, died age 16.
Right: Minnie May Hays Olive, Walker Cemetery #1, Cottage Grove, Tennessee, died age 72,

Left: Mary A. "Munsey" Hays, Hays Cemetery, Cottage Grove, Tennessee, died age 1.
Middle: Curtis Maxwell "Buck" Hays, Walker Cemetery #1, Cottage Grove, Tennessee, died age 69.
Right: Alma Lee Hays McVay Wallace, Maplewood Cemetery, Paris, Tennessee, died age 95.

Left: Ballie Hays, Hays Cemetery, Cottage Grove, Tennessee, died age 12.
Right: Naoma Hays, Hays Cemetery, Cottage Grove, Tennessee, died age 26.

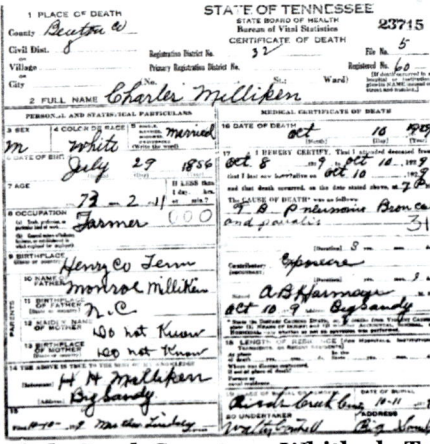

Monroe and Gillie Milliken's son, Charles John Milliken, Birds Creek Cemetery, Whitlock, Tennessee, died age 72; Charles Milliken death certificate.

Monroe and Gillie Milliken's grandsons. Left: Herman H. Milliken, Pleasant Ridge Cemetery, Big Sandy, Tennessee, died age 64. Right: Holmes C. Milliken, Walker Cemetery, Cottage Grove, Tennessee, died age 78.

Monroe and Gillie Milliken's granddaughter Josephine Eva Milliken Puryear, Walker Cemetery #1, Cottage Grove, Tennessee, died age 71.

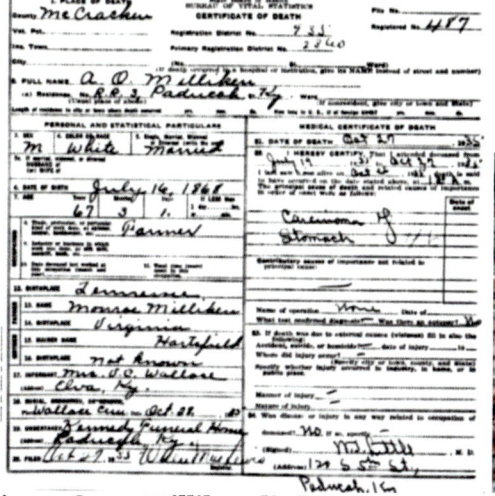

Monroe and Gillie Milliken's son. Left: Amos Oscar Milliken died age 67 and second spouse Mary R. Ward died age 84, Wallace Cemetery #1, Iola, Kentucky. Middle: A.O. Milliken death certificate. Right: Amos Oscar's first spouse, Anna Laura Fletcher Milliken, Milliken Cemetery, Tennessee, died age 25.

In the **1900 US Census,** Amos and Anna's children Guy (10) and Pearl (7) were listed as living in Marshall County, Kentucky, with [John] Bailey T. Milliken (1852-1929, their cousin, who was their Uncle George Melton Milliken's son). Their mother had died in 1894. Their father's whereabouts have not been determined for the year 1900. However, see 1910 US Census when Oscar was in Arkansas with his nephew, Bailey Milliken.

In the **1910 US Census,** Guy (20) was listed as living in Marshall County, Kentucky, with his aunt and uncle Emma N[ora Fletcher] (1862-1912, Emma was Guy's maternal aunt) and John D[ice] McGregor (1862-1916). Guy's occupation was a drug store clerk.

In the **1910 Caron's Paducah [Kentucky] Directory,** Guy W. Milliken is listed as a clerk at a business address of 503 Washington.

In the **1910 US Census,** Ina Pearl (18) was listed as living with her aunt and uncle in Marshall County, Kentucky with Ella M[illiken] (1861-1942, Pearl's Uncle George Melton Milliken's daughter, Pearl's cousin) and John H. Phillips (1853-1915) who were married 1881. A boarder, Victor Conrad Wallace (24) was listed as an RFD carrier. Pearl and Victor (1885-1949) would later marry (about 1914) and have 3 children.

33

**Monroe and Gillie Milliken's granddaughter Ina Pearl and Victor Wallace.
Buried Wallace Cemetery #1, Iola, Marshall County, Kentucky.**

In the **1910 US Census**, Oscar (widowed and occupation listed as a house carpenter) was living in Bayou Metro, Arkansas, as a boarder next to other Milliken family members: Ray (Bailey's son) and Ella Milliken, Don Milliken, Bailey Milliken (cousin), Lillian Milliken (cousin), and William (cousin) and Roxie and Anne Milliken.

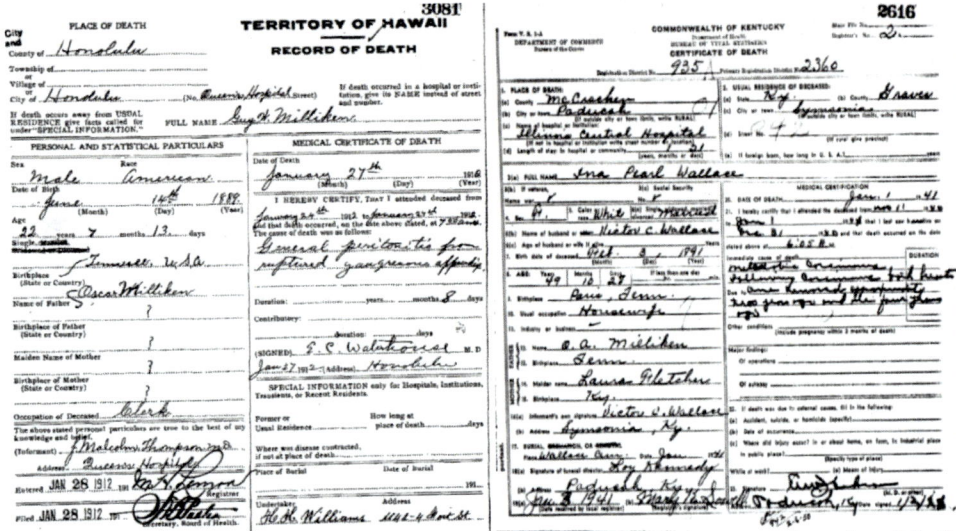

**Left: Guy W. Milliken (1889-1912) death certificate. Died at age 22 of "general peritonitis from rupture gangrenous appendix." It's unknown why he was in Hawaii. In the 1910 US Census he was living in Kentucky. Buried in Milliken Cemetery, Henry County, Tennessee.
Right: Ina Pearl Milliken Wallace (1891-1941) death certificate. Died at age 49 of metastatic carcinoma following breast cancer, two years and four years.**

**Left: Monroe and Gillie Milliken's son Amos (right) with his son Roy and Roy's spouse Mary, Kentucky, c. 1930.
Right: Roy Milliken, Forest Hill Cemetery-South, Memphis, Tennessee, died age 87.**

Left: Monroe and Gillie Milliken's son, George Simeon Milliken, Hartsfield Cemetery, Paris, Tennessee, died age 7 months. **Right:** Monroe and Sarah Milliken's daughter Roe Clark, Oak Hill Union Church Cemetery, Osage, Tennessee, died age 34.

~~~

The **1850 US Census** lists "Wm Monroe Milliken," 25, as a "farmer" living with "Gilly," 20, and their 3 children Thomas (5), Martha (3), and W.A. (1). Note that Monroe's parents, Amos and Elizabeth, live nearby with Monroe's brother George, 22, his wife Elvira, 20, and their daughter Susan, 7 months.

1850 US Census.

The **1850 US Federal Census—Slave Schedule** lists George M. Milliken with 3 black slaves (female, 20; males, 17 and 7 months). Wm. Monroe Milliken had 2 black slaves (male, 20; female, 15).

1850 US Federal Census—Slave Schedule.

The **1860 US Census** lists "W. W. "Melligan" with "Silla A." and 8 children, ages 14 to 8 months, in Henry County, Tennessee.

1860 US Census.

The **1860 US Federal Census—Slave Schedule** lists that George M. Milliken had 6 slaves (female, 32; male, 25; female, 20; male, 5; male 1; female, 1 month). W. M. Milliken had 5 slaves, four black and one "m" for mixed/mulatto (female, 36, "m"; male, 18; female, 15; female, 7, male, 3). Their mother Elizabeth Milliken had 3 slaves, two black and one mixed (male, 40; female, 16; male, 9, "m").

1860 US Federal Census—Slave Schedule.

The **1870 US Census** lists W.M. Milliken as a "farmer" with G. A. and 7 children, ages 18 to 6 months, in Henry County, Tennessee.

1870 US Census.

The **1880 US Census** lists William M. Milliken as a "farmer" living with Sarah (whom he married 1872 after Gillie's death) "keeping house" with Amos O., 13, "at school" along with two stepsons, Gova Cox, 24, and John Cox, 20, are both labeled as "works on farm."

1880 US Census.

~~~

Ballie Milliken is the Cook family ancestor.

~~~

Summary of Maternal Third Generation

Sarah Elizabeth "Ballie" Milliken Cook was born in Tennessee as the eighth of ten siblings. Her mother died when Ballie was 11 years old. Her father remarried when Ballie was 13, gaining her a stepmother and two stepbrothers.

She married Elias Power Cook, when she was 18, in Henry County, Tennessee. They had 6 children in 11 years. Their first child was born when Ballie was 23. The last child was born when Ballie was 34. Tera Monroe Cook (1882-1957), Rupert Berber Cook (1883-1961), Heber Amos Cook (1886-after 1919), Ruby Irma Cook Stover (1888-1975), Eric Power Cook (1890-1987), Gela Lela Cook (1893-1972).

Ballie's father, Monroe Milliken, died in 1896, when Ballie was 37. E. P. Cook, Ballie's husband, was the administrator of Monroe's estate. He compiled an inventory, sold items, and settled the estate from 1896 until 1899. Ballie received $10.33 as her part of the distribution.

Elias and Ballie moved with their children from Paris, Tennessee, to Independence, Missouri, in 1905, according to their son Eric. Elias P. Cook's obituary said that the family "located at Independence in 1895." The **1900 US Census** lists the Cook family as living in Tennessee.

Their granddaughter, Virginia, indicates that "my parents and grandparents—mother's family—left Kentucky-Tennessee to gather to Zion." RLDS Church members believed Zion was located in Jackson County, Missouri.

Ballie's husband died at home in 1919. In the **1920 US Census,** Ballie was shown living at 1028 West Maple Avenue, Independence, Missouri. There was a 17-year-old boarder living with Ballie named Charlote Shepherd. Her occupation was listed as "clerical, mail order house." There was also a couple who resided in the upstairs apartment: Enoch and Jewell Wisemore. His occupation was "fireman, railroad."

Ballie died in 1921 at the age of 61 from a brain tumor she'd had for 8 months. She's buried in Mound Grove Cemetery (Independence, Missouri).

Five of Ballie's children were alive at the time of her death (Heber's death date is unknown but after 1919). Those children lived to be from 75 to 97 years old. Two deaths were due to coronary occlusion and cancer of the pancreas. Two children were known to be diabetics and one had rheumatoid arthritis.

Gela Lela Cook is the Cook ancestor in the family. See details in Summary of Maternal/Paternal Second Generation.

~~~

Sarah Elizabeth "Ballie" Milliken Cook

Born 7 Oct 1859 (Paris, Tennessee); died 4 Oct 1921 at age 61 of a brain tumor (Independence, Missouri). Buried Mound Grove Cemetery (Independence, Missouri). Married Elias Power Cook (1842-1919) on 6 Dec 1877 (Henry County, Tennessee). Elias Power Cook's details are given under Paternal Cook Family. The children of Ballie and Elias are listed after his information in the Summary of Maternal/Paternal Second Generation.

Ballie Cook, location unknown, ~1910s.

Postcards to Ballie Cook, 1910–1919

Front: Saints' Home, Lamoni, Iowa. **Editor Note:** Located on 60 acres at the far north end of Silver Street in Lamoni. Built in 1896/1897 for $19,000, it opened in 1898 for the benefit of old folks. In September 1941, it was converted to a dormitory for men attending Graceland College and renamed North Hall. The designer of this building, Charles Dunham, was also the architect of the Graceland College Administration Building. North Hall became a dormitory for women in the fall of 1943. Other dormitories were built on the campus and this building was demolished about 1952.

Postmark: Lamoni, Iowa, Nov 11, 1910, 7:30 PM; 1 cent stamp

To: Mrs. Ballie Cook, 1028 W. Maple Ave, Independence, Missouri

Lamoni Iowa Nov 10-10

Dear Mama: I was very glad to get your card but of course did not count it an answer to my letter so I am expecting a letter any time now. I have not been feeling very well the last day or two. We [Graceland College, opened in 1895] are to have the game of the season next Saturday with Leon [Iowa]. The other score was five to five. I got a card from Guy [probably Eric's cousin, Guy W. Milliken, who was a year older than Eric and living in Kentucky at this time] a day or two ago. He said he would soon write. Hoping to hear from you soon. I am your loving son. Eric [Cook, Ballie's 20-year-old son]

~~~

Front: Lincoln Park, Chicago, Illinois. **Editor Note:** It is a 1,208-acre park along Lake Michigan. Originally named Cemetery Park and then Lake Park in 1860, it was renamed in 1865 for US President Abraham Lincoln. It is the city's largest public park. The park is well-known for the Lincoln Park Zoo, a free zoo open year-round, and the Lincoln Park Conservatory. It also is home to the Alfred Caldwell Lily Pool and the Chicago History Museum.

Postmark: Milwaukee, Wis., Aug 17, 1911, 3:39 PM; 1 cent stamp

To: Mrs. E. P. Cook, Independence, 1028 W. Maple Ave. Mo.

8-17-11 11:16 A.M. Aboard Steam Ship "[Christopher] Columbus" for Milwaukee from Chicago. Trip is fine—wish you could be with me. Guy [probably Guy W. Milliken, Ballie's 21-year-old nephew] Written on front: Went through this yesterday eve. Guy

Editor Note: The SS *Christopher Columbus* was an American excursion liner on the Great Lakes, in service between 1893 and 1933. She was the only whaleback ship ever built for passenger service. The ship was designed by Alexander McDougall, the developer and promoter of the whaleback design.

~~~

Front: U.S. Capitol from Library of Congress, Washington, D.C. **Editor Note:** The United States Capitol, set on a height overlooking the amphitheater of the Potomac, is one of the larges and stateliest buildings in the world. It is 751 feet in length and 350 feet in width, covering three and a half acres. The statue of Freedom on the dome towers 307 feet above the esplanade. The corner stone was laid by President Washington in 1793, the central building was finished in 1797; and the extensions were first occupied by Congress in 1857 and 1859.

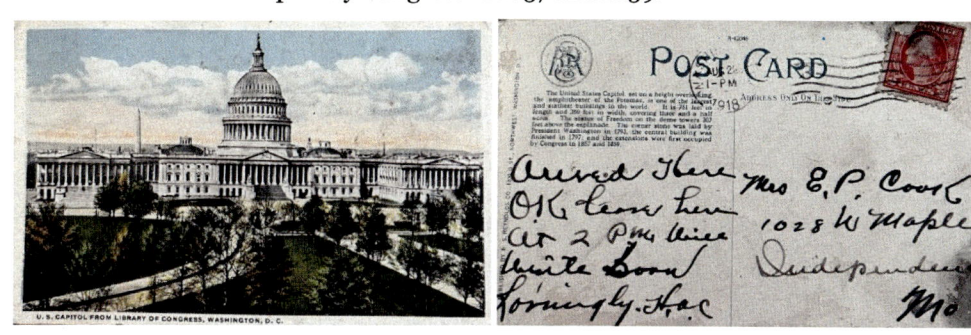

Postmark: Washington, D.C., Aug 22, 1918, 1 PM; 2 cent stamp

To: Mrs. E. P. Cook, 1028 W Maple, Independence, Mo

Arrived Here OK. Leave here at 2 PM. Will write soon.

Lovingly, H.A.C [Heber Amos Cook, Ballie's 32-year-old son]

Editor Note: Heber registered for the World War 1 draft in 1918 at the age of 32. The last known mention of him was a year after this postcard in a November 1919 letter, when he was probably living in Fulton, Kentucky. It's unknown when, how, and where he died.

~~~

Front: 7685. Eagle Cliff on Mt. Manitou Scenic Incline, Manitou, Colo. MOUNT MANITOU PARK. This is a beautiful natural mountain park of a thousand acres, with ten miles of trails, 9,500 feet above sea level. The finest trip and grandest view in the Rockies. Ten thousand square miles of scenery. The Mt. Manitou Scenic Incline is the longest, highest and greatest railway of its kind in the world. A rise of one-half mile elevation in a ride of one and one-quarter miles.

Postmark: Murray, KY, Jun 18, 1919, 7 PM; 2 cent stamp

To: Mrs. E. P. Cook. Cottage. Grove, Tenn, Route 2, Box. 18,

June 18 1919

Dear Ballie, I got your letter yesterday [in Colorado]. I haven't heard from home [Missouri?]. No rain since the 12, haveing hot weather. I am at Bro Bauses [John George Baus (1895-1972)]. Mollie [Amalie Baus (1901-1953)] has been canning berries. I don't know when I will go to Murray [Kentucky]. I will have to go back to Bro Bascoms [Walker and Belle Bascom in Independence, Missouri?] this week. As soon as I have time I will write you a letter, and tell about my visit. The girls [Lizzie's daughters?] are going to Mayfield [Tennessee?] to and I will go with them. love to you, Lizzie

Editor Note: Ballie and E. P. Cook and their children lived in Murray, Kentucky, before they moved to Independence, Missouri, in 1905. Ballie's sister, Eugenia "Jennie" Porter Milliken Shell Hays, lived in Cottage Grove, Tennessee. Perhaps Ballie was visiting Jennie when she received this postcard. Lizzie might be Mary Elizabeth Howard Cook (1856-1944), Ballie's sister-in-law, who was married to E.P. Cook's brother, David Washington Cook (1846-1903).

~~~

Ballie M. Cook death certificate. She died at age 61 of a brain tumor that she had for eight months. The informant was "B. Cook"—perhaps her son Berber. The maiden name of Ballie's mother was given as "Gilly Edmonds," however, Gillie's maiden name was Hartsfield.

~~~

Paternal Cook Family

Color Coding for Paternal Cook Names

The following color coding has been used to help readers trace the generations. The first generation is listed as our mother's generation.

First generation: parents, aunts, uncles

Second generation: grandparents, great-aunts, great-uncles

Third generation: great-grandparents

Fourth generation: great-great-grandparents

Fifth generation

Virginia Moorman's mother was Gela Lela Cook Moorman.

Gela Moorman's father was Elias Power "E.P." Cook.

E.P. Cook's parents were Edmund and Mary Ann O'Brien Cook.

Edmund Cook's parents were **Wesley** and **Elizabeth Cook.**

Mary Ann O'Brien Cook's parents were **John Joseph** and **Mary O'Brien.**

~~~

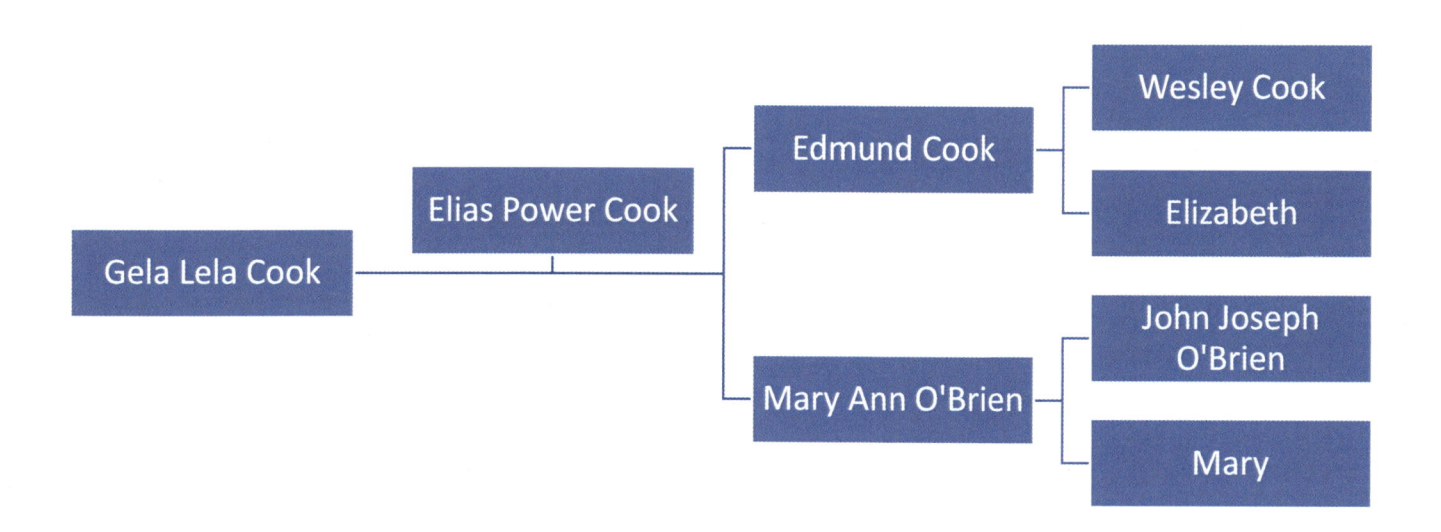

Cook Paternal Family Ancestor Locations

Ireland, Dublin, ~1775: John Joseph O'Brien birth, Gela's great-grandfather
Virginia, Pittsylvania County, on North Carolina border, ~1784-1840: Wesley R. Cook birth and death, Gela's great-grandfather
Virginia, Pittsylvania County, 1805: Edmund Cook birth, Gela's grandfather
Ireland, Dublin, 1812: Mary Ann O'Brien birth, Gela's grandmother
1821: O'Brien family immigrated to US
North Carolina, Caswell County, on Virginia border, 1830: Edmund and Mary Ann O'Brien Cook marriage
Kentucky, Russell County, 90 miles east of Bowling Green, 1836: Elizabeth A. Cook death, Gela's great-grandmother
Virginia, 1842: Elias Power Cook birth, Gela's father
Kentucky, Calloway County, 40 miles south of Paducah, moved about 1845; 1850, 1860, 1870 US Census: Edmund and Mary Ann Cook. Virginia to Kentucky is about 600 miles.
Tennessee, Union City, 60 miles from Calloway County, Kentucky, 1861: Elias Cook enlisted in Confederate Army, wounded and crippled in a battle
Kentucky, New Concord, Calloway County, 1872: Edmund Cook death
Tennessee, 1877: Elias and Sarah Elizabeth "Ballie" Milliken Cook married
Tennessee, Paris, 25 miles from New Concord, Kentucky, 1882-1900: Elias Cook family. Calloway County, Kentucky, to Paris, Tennessee, is about 30 miles.
Tennessee Legislature, 1891-1892: Elias Cook served
Kentucky, New Concord, 1895: Mary Ann O'Brien death
Missouri, Independence, 1910: Elias Cook family, US Census Paris, Tennessee, to Independence, Missouri, is about 500 miles.
Missouri, Independence, 1919: Elias Cook death

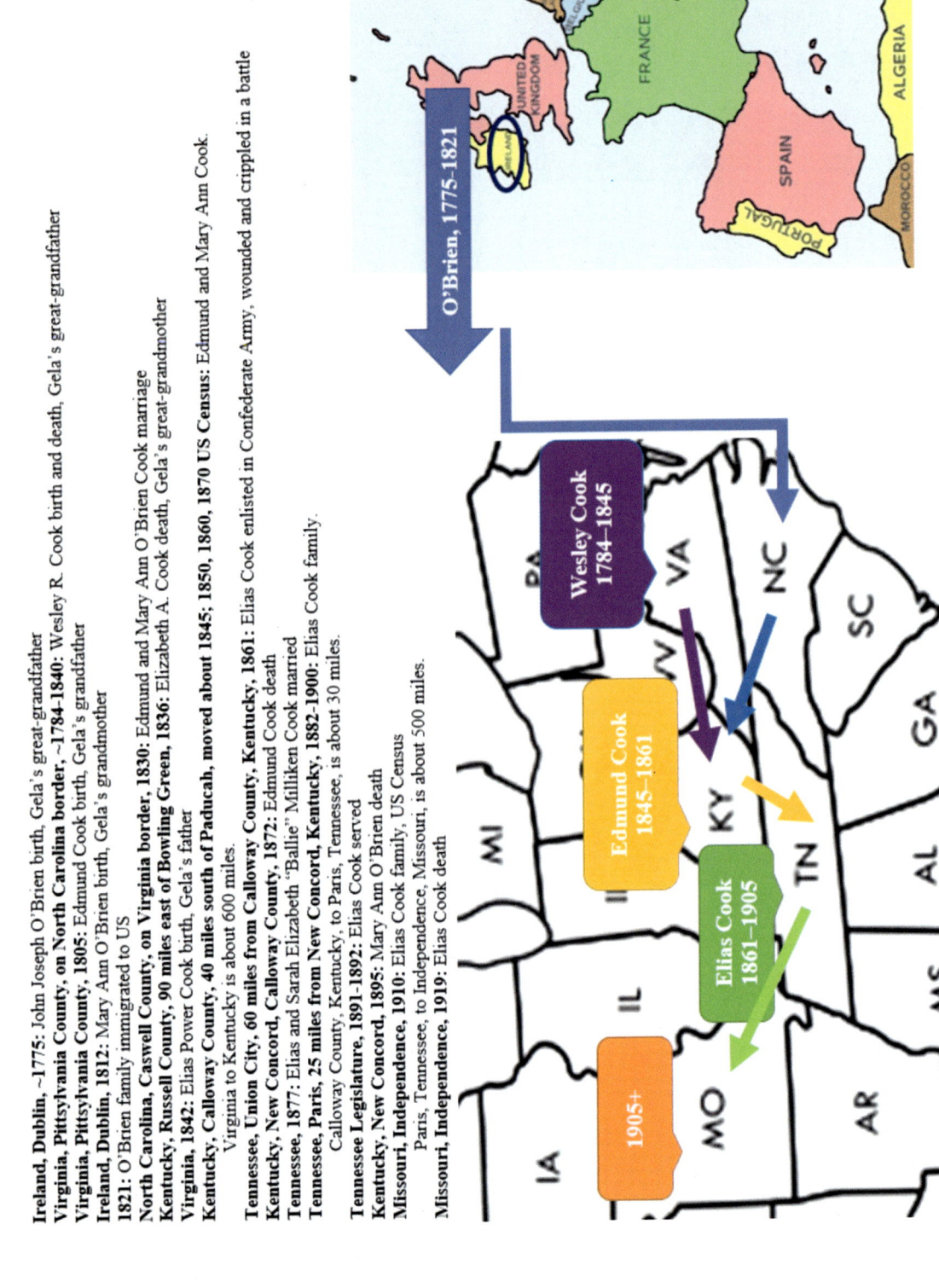

Summary of Paternal Fifth Generation

Little is known about **Wesley and Elizabeth Cook.** No census records or military records have been found. Wesley was born and died in Virginia. It's unknown when and where he married Elizabeth. Their son Edmund was born in Virginia in 1805, but at some time after that, the family moved to Kentucky. Elizabeth died in Kentucky in 1836 and four years later (1840) Wesley died in Virginia. In 1850, Edmund was living in Kentucky. No gravesites are known for Wesley or Elizabeth.

Edmund Cook is the Cook family ancestor. See details in the Paternal Fourth Generation.

~~~

Little is known about **John and Mary O'Brien.** John was born in Ireland and Mary was born in England. They both died in North Carolina. It's unknown when they moved to the United States, but it was after 1818, when the last of their six children was born in Ireland, and before 1830 when John's name appears in the US Census. Two of their children died in Virginia, one died in South Carolina, and one died in Kentucky, so the O'Brien family was in various locations on the East Coast.

Mary Ann O'Brien is the Cook family ancestor. See details in the Paternal Fourth Generation.

~~~

Wesley Cook

Born ~1784 (Pittsylvania County, Virginia); died 1 Jan 1840 at age 60 (Pittsylvania County, Virginia). Unknown burial location. Unknown marriage details. Wesley's parents unknown.

~~~

Elizabeth Cook

Born ~1780 (unknown location); died 1836 about age 56 (Russell County, Kentucky). Unknown burial location. Unknown marriage details, but probably before 1805 in Virginia, as her son was born in Jul 1805. Elizabeth's parents unknown.

~~~

Edmund Cook is the Cook family ancestor. See details in the Paternal Fourth Generation.

~~~

John Joseph O'Brien

Born ~1775 (Dublin, Ireland); died after 1850 (Caswell County, North Carolina). Unknown marriage details but probably married before 1807 in Ireland. John's parents unknown.

In 1812, his daughter Mary Ann was born in Dublin, Ireland. In 1816, his daughter Catherine was born in Cork, Ireland, a distance of about 160 miles from Dublin. It's not known when John and Mary and the six children immigrated to the United States. It might have been after 1818 (when their last child was born in Ireland) and before 1830 (when they possibly appear in the US Census).

In the **1830 US Census,** Joseph Obrian [sic] had 3 males (10-14), 1 male (50-59), 1 female (15-19), and 1 female (40-49), along with 2 slaves, living in Caswell County, North Carolina. This might include him, his wife, 3 sons (Joseph, John, Thomas), and 1 daughter (Catherine).

In the **1840 US Census,** Jos C Brien [sic] had 1 male (60-69), 1 female (20-29), 1 female (50-59), and 1 slave living in Caswell County, North Carolina. This might include him, his wife, and his daughter Catherine.

In the **1850 US Census,** Joseph O Brian [sic], 75, farmer, born in Ireland, was living in Caswell County, North Carolina, with his wife Mary O Brian [sic], 60, born in London, and his daughter Catherian [sic], 31, born in Dublin.

1850 US Census

~~~

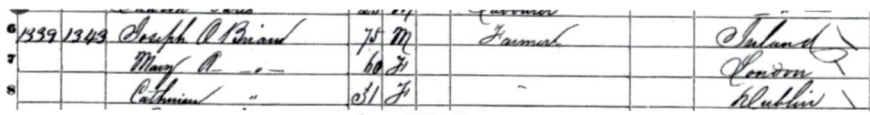

Mary O'Brien

Born ~1790 (London, England); died after 1850 (Caswell County, North Carolina). Unknown marriage details but probably married before 1807 in Ireland. It's not know when Mary left London and moved to Ireland. Mary's parents unknown. In 1850, Mary lived in Caswell County, North Carolina.

Mary Ann O'Brien is the Cook family ancestor. See details in the Paternal Fourth Generation.

~~~

Summary of John and Mary O'Brien Family

John and Mary had 6 children in 11 years, all were born in Ireland.

1. Joseph Washington O'Brien (~1807/1815, Ireland-?).

2. Hannah O'Brien Tyree (~1810, Ireland-1880, Pittsylvania County, Virginia) married David Augustine Tyree (~1807-after 1895) on 6 Apr 1830 (Caswell County, North Carolina). They had 7 children: *Mary A. Tyree* (1836-1923), *Sarah Jane Tyree Webb* (1838-1912), *Thomas Martin Tyree* (1840-1902), *David Augustine Tyree* (1842-1908), *Hannah Adelaide "Addie" Tyree* (1845-1920), *William P. Tyree* (1850-1907), *Catharine E. Tyree* (1852-1856).

Hannah's spouse David was listed as a bridge keeper in the 1850 US Census and as a carpenter in the 1860 and the 1870 US Census. Mary was listed as a teacher in the 1860 US Census. The son David served as a captain in the Southern Confederacy for three years. William also served in the Confederacy.

3. Mary Ann O'Brien Cook (23 Jul/Dec 1812, Dublin, Ireland-19 Feb 1895, Kentucky). See details in the Paternal Fourth Generation.

4. Catherine O'Brien (15 Jul 1814, Cork, Ireland-after 1880). In the 1880 US Census, Catherine was living with her brother John and his family in Dan River, Caswell, North Carolina.

5. John Magnus O'Brien, Dr. (1816, Ireland-5 Mar 1905, Danville, Virginia) married Elizabeth Ann "Annie" Leary (1835, North Carolina-after 1880) on 27 Feb 1859 (Macon, Georgia). They had 3 children: *Emma F. O'Brien* (1864-after 1880), *Willie W. O'Brien* (1866-after 1880), *Thomas "Tommie" Marshall O'Brien* (1869-1952), all born in Alabama. John married Ann Morning Blair on 29 Nov 1871 (Caswell, North Carolina).

In the 1870 US Census, John O'Brien is 48 and listed as a nonpracticing physician. The value of his personal estate is listed at $20,000. The family is living in Muscogee, Georgia. John's birthplace is listed as Virginia. Elizabeth's birthplace is listed as Georgia. The three children were listed as born in Alabama. Mary J, Wiggins, a 22-year-old mulatto "domestic," was living with the family.

6. Thomas Marshall O'Brien (1818, Ireland-1844, Charleston, South Carolina).

~~~

Mary Ann O'Brien is the Cook family ancestor. See details in the Paternal Fourth Generation.

~~~

Summary of Paternal Fourth Generation

Edmund Cook was born in Virginia. When he was 25, he married Mary Ann O'Brien in North Carolina. He was 26 when his first child was born and 48 when his last child was born.

Edmund died in 1872 in Kentucky at age 67 and was survived by 10 of his 12 children. Two daughters died before he did (in 1854 and 1861). Edmund is buried at the Cook Cemetery in New Concord, Kentucky.

Mary Ann O'Brien was born in Ireland. She arrived in the US in 1821 about age 8. She married Edmund Cook when she was 17 and had her first child at age 19. Her last child was born when she was 41. Mary Ann died in 1895 in Kentucky at age 82 and was survived by 9 of her 12 children (a son died in 1891). Mary Ann is buried at the Cook Cemetery in New Concord, Kentucky.

Edmund and Mary Ann were married in North Carolina (probably where Mary Ann was living). However, 7 of their children were born in Virginia (1831-1844) and 5 of their children were born in Kentucky (1846-1853). It appears that they moved from Virginia to Calloway County, Kentucky about 1845.

Edmund and Mary Ann's children died at ages 1 year to 87 years. Two children preceded Edmund in death: Charlotte in 1861 at age 23 and Virginia in 1854 at age 1. Another child preceded Mary Ann in death: John died in 1891 at age 44.

There were a variety of causes of death including pneumonia (Williamson and Edmund), abdominal tumor (Susan), senility (Hannah and Mary Anne), prostate cancer (Thomas), and kidney disease (Virginia).

~~~

Elias Power Cook is the Cook family ancestor. See details in the Paternal Third Generation.

~~~

Edmund Cook

Born 12 Jul 1805 (Pittsylvania County, Virginia); died 9 Sep 1872 at age 67 (New Concord, Kentucky). Buried Cook Cemetery (New Concord, Kentucky). Married Mary Ann O'Brien 15 Feb 1830 (Caswell County, North Carolina).

Edmund Cook, 1805-1872, died age 67. Picture on right courtesy of Beth Boyle.

~~~

Mary Ann O'Brien Cook

Born 23 Dec 1812 (Ireland); died 19 Feb 1895 (New Concord, Kentucky). Arrived in US in 1821, about 8 years old. Buried Cook Cemetery (New Concord, Kentucky). Headstone is no longer standing. Married Edmund Cook in 1830 (North Carolina).

Birth Register of Mary O'Brien, 1812.

Mary Ann O'Brien Cook, 1812-1895, died age 82. Picture on right courtesy of Beth Boyle.

~~~

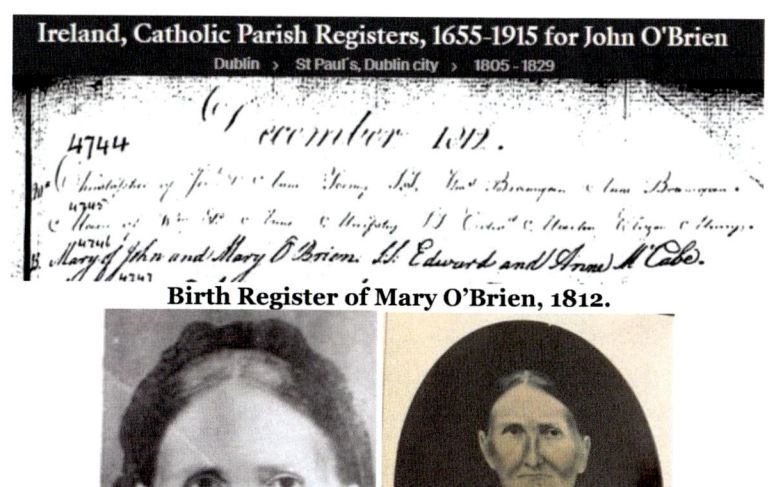

Summary of Edmund and Mary Ann Cook Family

Edmund (25) married Mary Ann (17) on 15 Feb 1830 (Caswell, North Carolina). They had 12 children in 22 years.

1. **Joseph/Joe Wesley Cook** (6 Apr 1831, Virginia-2 May 1901, Murray, Kentucky). Buried West Fork Baptist Church Cemetery (Murray, Kentucky). Married Hannah Wimberley Cook (1843-1910) on 19 Jan 1867 (Paris, Tennessee). They had 8 children: **Louisa Florence Cook** (1867-1941), **John Madison Cook** (1869-1953), **Nellie Ann Frances Cook Woods** (1872-1954), **Joetta Cook** (1875-1956), **Robert Walter Cook** (1877-1966), **Lillian Etha Cook** (1880-1967), **Myrtle Cook** (1883-1883), **Gertie Cleveland Cook Sledd** (1884-1956).

2. **Williamson/William M./W.M. Cook** (1 Jun 1834, Virginia-9 Feb 1908, McConnell, Tennessee). Died of pneumonia. Buried in Fairview Cemetery (Fulton, Kentucky). Married Jennette Rebecca Owen Cook (1838-1919) on 22 May 1859 (Kentucky). They had 8 children: **Robert Ernest Cook** (1860-1876), **Diana Elizabeth Cook Rankin** (1861-1948), **Mary Mildred Cook Locke** (1865-1909), **Nellie Leona Cook Rankin** (1869-1945), **Minenra Silma Cook** (1870-1871), **William Owen Cook** (1872-1940), **Edmund Curtis Cook** (1874-1957), **Minnie Alice Cook Powers** (1879-1962).

3. **Susan Catherine Cook Waters** (21 Apr 1835, Caswell County, Virginia-30 Sep 1913, Calloway County, Kentucky). Died of "malnutrition result of abdominal tumor and senility." Buried at Murray City Cemetery (Murray, Kentucky). Married John Jefferson Waters (1827-1875) on 8 Mar 1854 (North Carolina). John served in the Confederate 2nd Kentucky Calvary, Calloway County, in the US Civil War for about 3 years. Buried at Cook Cemetery (New Concord, Kentucky). They had 8 children: **Robert Alexander Waters** (1856-1859), **Martha Ann Rebecca "Mattie" Waters Ligon** (1857-1948), **Mary Francie "Mollie" Waters** (1860-1909), **Susan Carter Waters Whitnell** (1861-1951), **Edmund Reason Waters** (1866-1868), **Alice Green Waters** (1868-1959), **David Lee "Willie" Waters,** (1870-1955), **Richard Wesley "Rich" Waters** (1872-1962). Martha and Mary were schoolteachers. Alice worked as a First Methodist Church missionary in China.

4. **Charlotte J. Cook** (5 Oct 1838, Virginia-20 Nov 1861, Cherry Corner, Kentucky. Buried Cook Cemetery (Murray, Kentucky). Died age 23.

5. **Edmund James/EJ Cook** (25 May 1840, Danville, Virginia-12 Dec 1927, Cherry Corner, Kentucky). Served as a US Confederate soldier. Enlisted 13 Sep 1861 (age 21) at Union City, Tennessee. Corporal, Thirty-Third Infantry. Died of pneumonia. Buried Hicks Cemetery (Calloway County, Kentucky). Married Susan Jane Lassiter Cook (1846-1902) on 28 Nov 1867. They had 8 children: **Lemuel Anthis Cook** (1868-1954), **Albert Wilson Cook** (1871-1885), **Lurena Cook** (1873-1951), **Adella "Della" Cook Swann** (1875-1948), **Daisy Hunter Cook** (1877-1879), **Edmund Linn Cook** (1879-1960), **Charles Blakely Cook** (1884-1884), **Gordon Obrien Cook** (1884-1973).

6. **Elias Power/E.P. Cook** (6 Apr 1842, Virginia-12 May 1919, Independence, Missouri). See details in Paternal Third Generation.

7. **Hannah H. Cook Ryan** (27 Apr 1844, Virginia-18 Nov 1928, Murray, Kentucky). Died of "senility—nothing else visible to report" secondary to fall. Buried Murray City Cemetery (Murray, Kentucky). Married William Ryan (1828-1896) in 1883 (Kentucky). Two sons: **William Thomas Ryan** (1884-1929), **John Graves Ryan** (1888-1962). William died at age 44 due to "heart trouble brought on by heavy drinking moonshine found dead." John was the city attorney in Murray, Kentucky, for 18 years.

8. **David Washington Cook** (22 Feb 1846, Cherry Corner, Kentucky-9 Jul 1903, Sedalia, Kentucky). Buried Lebanon Church of Christ Cemetery, Sedalia, Kentucky. Married Mary Elizabeth Howard Cook (1856-1944) on 14 Jan 1875 (Paris, Tennessee). They had 12 children: **William/Willie Carlton Cook** (1875-1965), **Eula May Cook Roberts** (1878-1970), **Hattie Jeanette Cook** (1880-1975), **Charles/Charlie Boswell Cook** (1882-1979), **Roxy Cleo Cook Casey** (1884-1989), **Guy David Cook** (1884-1969), **Bessie Jo Cook Hill** (1886-1966), **Marjorie/Margie Primrose Cook Mills** (1888-1978), **Lillie Ella Cook Cooper** (1890-1988), **Ralph Leonard Cook** (1892-1990), **Mary Lane Cook** (1896-1980), **Marion Cook** (1899-1899). Roxy and Guy were twins. Virginia Dungan's notes mention that Hattie lived with Mary, who was blind, and "lived x street on Maple," Independence, Missouri.

9. **John G. Cook** (5 Oct 1847, Kentucky-1891, Cairo, Illinois). In the **1870 US Census,** John lived with his sister, Susan Waters. His occupation was a farmer.

10. **Mary Anne M. Cook Grogan** (7 Jun 1849, Kentucky-11 Aug 1932, Calloway County, Kentucky). Died of "senility." Buried Murray City Cemetery, Kentucky. Married Dr. Rufus Lafayette Grogan (1836-1918) about 1890 (his second marriage). They had 1 child: **Hallet Elwin Grogan** (1891-1960).

11. Thomas Phoenix Cook (18 Jun 1851, Kentucky-2 Sep 1934, Hopkinsville, Kentucky). Died of "cancer of prostate." Buried at Murray City Cemetery (Kentucky). Married Sue Walker Holton Cook (1862-1941) in 1882. They had 6 children: *Hattie May Cook* (1885-1968), *Laura Maude Cook* (1887-1945), *Holton Cook* (1889-1969), *Thomas Diltz Cook* (1892-1953), *Granville Marr Cook* (1893-1968), *Denwell Cook* (1897-1910). Thomas was a judge: Honorable Thomas Phoenix Cook.

12. Virginia Frances Cook (24 Sep 1853, Kentucky-14 Oct 1854, Cherry Corner, Kentucky). Died of "disease of kidney" at age 1. Buried Cook Cemetery (New Concord, Kentucky).

~~~

Left: Edmund and Mary Ann Cook's son Joseph Wesley Cook, West Fork Baptist Church Cemetery, Murray, Kentucky, died age 70.
Middle: Edmund and Mary Ann Cook's granddaughter Nellie Cook Woods, Chapel Hill Cemetery, Mayfield, Kentucky, died age 81.
Right: Gertie Cleveland Cook Sledd, West Fork Baptist Church Cemetery, Murray, Kentucky, died age 72.

~~~

Edmund and Mary Ann Cook's son William Cook, Fairview Cemetery, Fulton, Kentucky, died age 72.
Middle: death card. Right: *Gospel Advocate*, 26 Mar 1908.

Edmund and Mary Ann Cook's grandchildren. Left: William Owen Cook, Fairview Cemetery, Fulton, Kentucky, died age 67.
Middle: Edmund Curtis Cook, Walnut Grove Cemetery, South Fulton, Tennessee, died age 83.
Right: Minnie Alice Cook Powers, Fairview Cemetery, Fulton, Kentucky, died age 81.

~~~

Edmund and Mary Ann's daughter Susan Catherine Cook Waters (1835-1913) with 5 of her 8 children. Top row: Carter, Mollie, Alice. Front row: Lee, Susan (mother), Richard. Not pictured: Mattie. Two sons died as toddlers. Location unknown. Picture after 1890, before 1909. Courtesy Beth Boyle.

Edmund and Mary Ann Cook's daughter Susan Catherine Cook Waters application for Confederate pension due to her spouse (John Jefferson Waters) serving during the US Civil War.

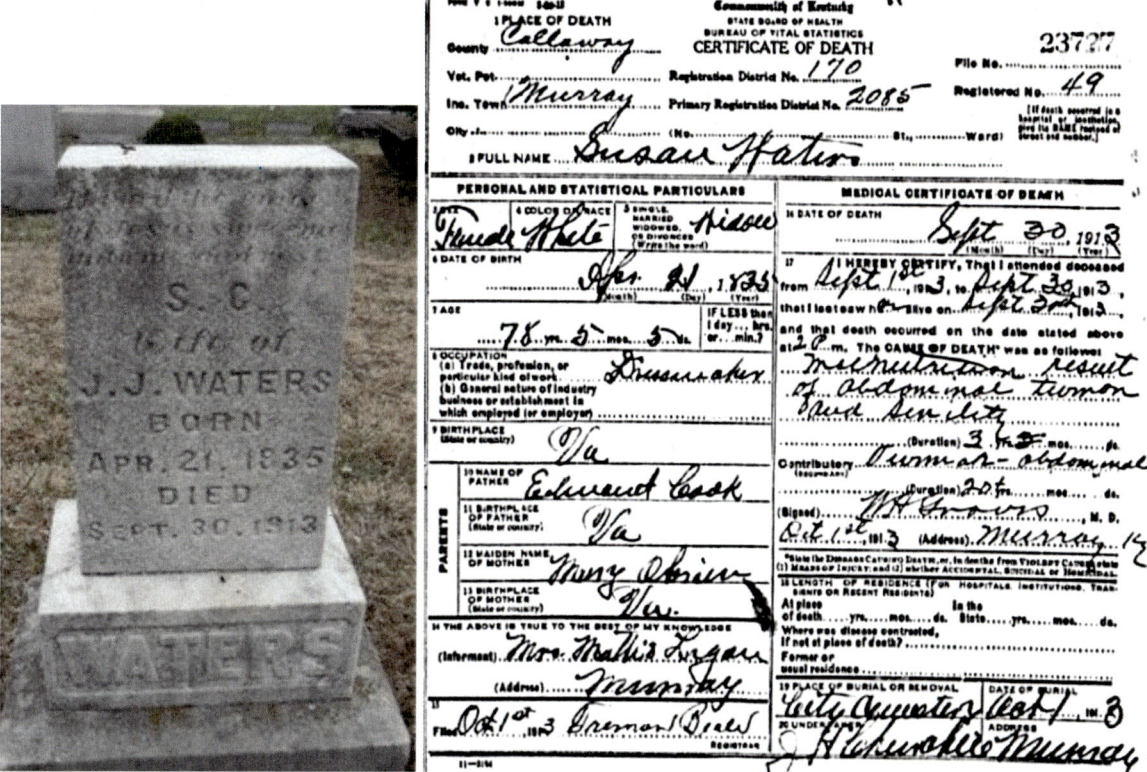

Edmund and Mary Ann Cook's daughter Susan Waters, Murray City Cemetery, Murray, Kentucky, died age 78. Death certificate informant was her daughter, Mattie Ligon.

Edmund and Mary Ann Cook's grandchildren. Upper row, left to right: Martha Ann Rebecca "Mattie" Waters Ligon died age 90, Mary F. Waters died age 49, Alice Green Waters died age 90. Lower row, left to right: Davie Lee Waters died age 84, Richard Wesley Waters died age 89. All buried Murray City Cemetery, Murray, Kentucky.

~~~

Left: Edmund and Mary Ann Cook's son Edmund James Cook and Susan Jane Lassiter Cook. Location and date unknown. Courtesy Beth Boyle. **Right:** Edmund and Mary Ann's son Edmund James and Susan Cook with 5 of their 8 children. Top: Lurena, Lemuel, Adella. Front: Edmund, EJ (father), Gordon, Susan (mother). Not pictured: Albert, Daisy, Charles (all deceased). Location unknown, circa 1890. Courtesy Beth Boyle.

Edmund and Mary Ann Cook's son. Left: Edmund James Cook, Hicks Cemetery, Calloway County, Kentucky, died age 87. **Right:** Edmund J. Cook death certificate.

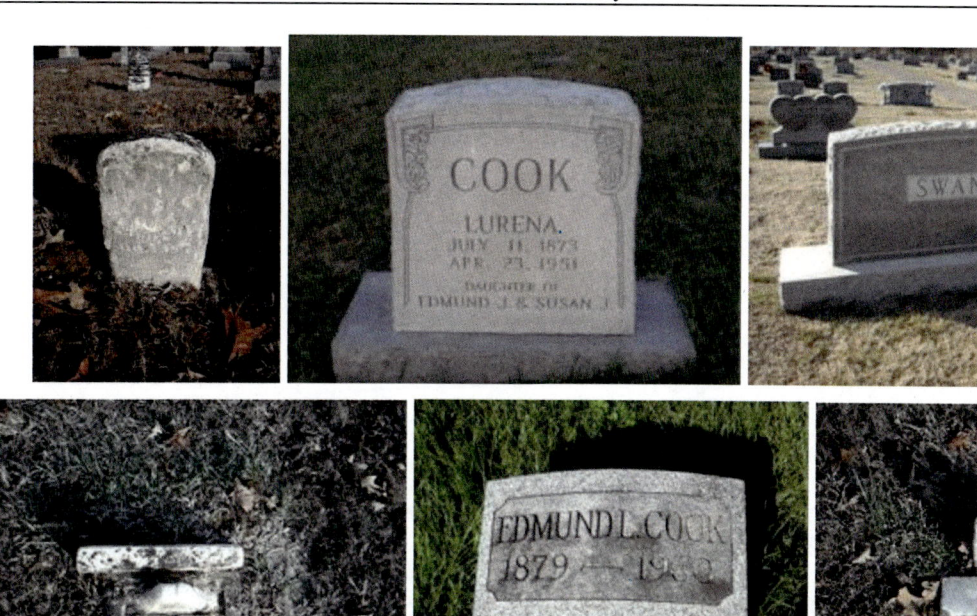

Edmund and Mary Ann Cook's grandchildren. Upper row, left to right: Albert Wilson Cook, Hicks Cemetery, Calloway County, Kentucky, died age 13; Lurena Cook, Hicks Cemetery, died age 77; Adella "Della" Cook Swann, Murray City Cemetery, Murray, Kentucky, died age 72. Lower row, left to right: Daisy Cook, Hicks Cemetery, died age 1; Edmund Linn Cook, Masonic Cemetery of Farmington South, Farmington, Missouri, died age 81; Charles Cook, Hicks Cemetery, died age 3 months.

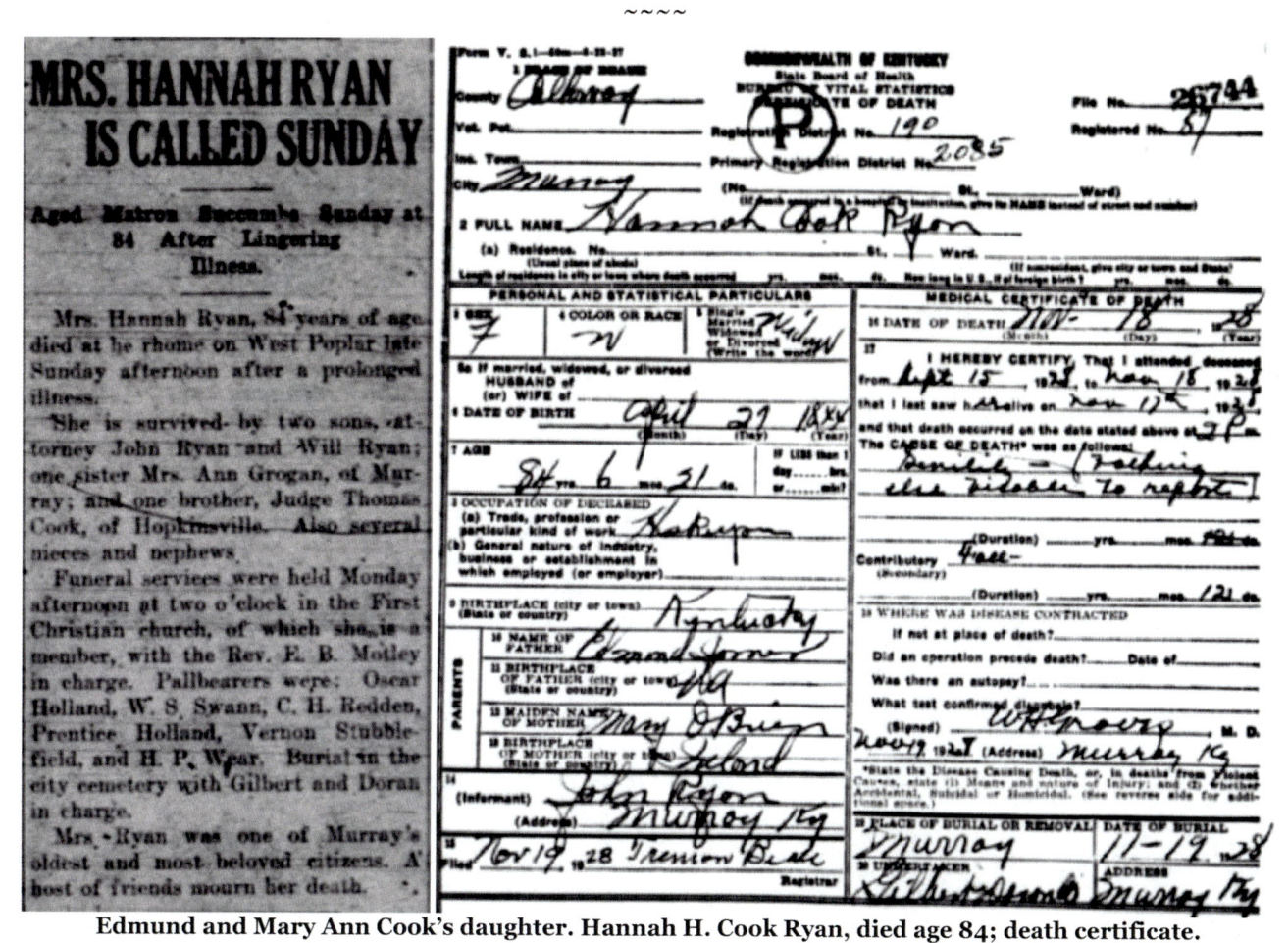

~~~~

MRS. HANNAH RYAN IS CALLED SUNDAY

Aged Matron Succumbs Sunday at 84 After Lingering Illness.

Mrs. Hannah Ryan, 84 years of age, died at her home on West Poplar late Sunday afternoon after a prolonged illness.

She is survived by two sons, attorney John Ryan and Will Ryan; one sister Mrs. Ann Grogan, of Murray; and one brother, Judge Thomas Cook, of Hopkinsville. Also several nieces and nephews.

Funeral services were held Monday afternoon at two o'clock in the First Christian church, of which she is a member, with the Rev. E. B. Motley in charge. Pallbearers were: Oscar Holland, W. S. Swann, C. H. Redden, Prentice Holland, Vernon Stubblefield, and H. P. Wear. Burial in the city cemetery with Gilbert and Doran in charge.

Mrs. Ryan was one of Murray's oldest and most beloved citizens. A host of friends mourn her death.

Edmund and Mary Ann Cook's daughter. Hannah H. Cook Ryan, died age 84; death certificate.

51

Edmund and Mary Ann Cook's son David Washington Cook and Mary Elizabeth Howard Cook.

David Washington Cook and Mary Elizabeth Howard Cook family. Back row: left to right: Mary, Roxy, Ralph, Lillie, Guy, Margie, Bessie. Front row: left to right: Charlie, Hattie, Mary Elizabeth, Eula, Willie. Mary Elizabeth Cook's house, Lee's Summit Road, Independence, Missouri, 21 August 1921.

Edmund and Mary Ann Cook's son. Left: David Washington Cook, Lebanon Church of Christ Cemetery, Sedalia, Kentucky, died age 57.
Right: David's spouse Mary Elizabeth Howard Cook, Mound Grove Cemetery, Independence, died age 88.

Edmund and Mary Ann Cook's grandchildren. Left and middle: Willie Carlton Cook.
Right: Eula May Cook Roberts, Mound Grove Cemetery, Independence, Missouri, died age 92.

Edmund and Mary Ann Cook's grandchildren. Left: Hattie (left) and Mary, who was blind.
Right: Hattie Jeanette Cook, Mound Grove Cemetery, Independence, Missouri, died age 95.

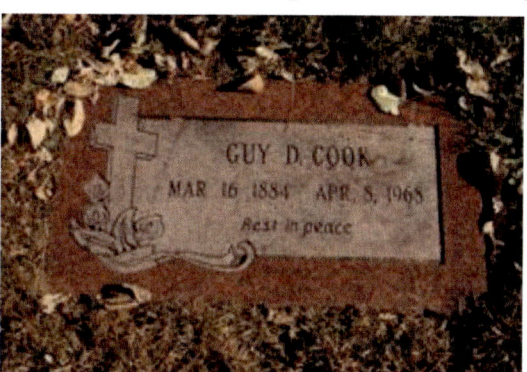

Edmund and Mary Ann Cook's grandsons. Left: Charles Boswell Cook died age 97.
Right: Guy D. Cook, Mound Grove Cemetery, Independence, Missouri, died age 85.

Edmund and Mary Ann Cook's granddaughters. Left: Bessie Jo Cook Hill, Silver Lake Cemetery, Ayrshire, Iowa, died age 79. Middle and right: Margie Primrose Cook Mills, Oak Grove Cemetery, Oak Grove, Missouri, died age 90.

Edmund and Mary Ann Cook's grandchildren. Left: Lillie Ella Cook Cooper died age 98. **Middle:** Ralph Leonard Cook died age 98. Both buried Mound Grove Cemetery, Independence, Missouri. **Right:** Mary Lane Cook.

~~~

Edmund and Mary Ann Cook's daughter. Left: Mary Anne Cook Grogan, Murray City Cemetery, Murry, Kentucky, died age 83.
Right: Edmund and Mary Ann Cook's granddaughter Hallett Elwin Grogan, Murray City Cemetery, Murray, Kentucky, died age 69.

~~~

Edmund and Mary Ann Cook's son Thomas Phoenix Cook, Murray City Cemetery, Kentucky, died age 83.

Edmund and Mary Ann Cook's grandson. Left: Holton Cook visa to Brazil, 1945. **Right:** Holton Cook, Walden Forest Oaks Memorial Park, Austin, Texas, died age 80.

Edmund and Mary Ann Cook's grandson Granville Marr "Randall" Cook, Holy Cross Cemetery, Brook Park, Ohio, died age 74.

~~~

The **1850 US Census** lists Edmund and his son Joseph as "farmers" living in Calloway County, Kentucky, with his wife and 10 children. Mary Ann was unable to read or write.

1850 US Census.

The **1850 US Federal Census—Slave Schedule** lists that Edmond Cook had 2 black slaves (female, 28, and female, 13).

1850 US Federal Census—Slave Schedule.

The **1860 US Census** lists Edmund as a "farmer" and Mary Ann as a "housewife" living in Calloway County, Kentucky, with 7 children. Also living with the Cook family was Dr. A. J. Smith, 19, medical, and A. Bannister, 25, laborer.

1860 US Census.

The **1860 US Federal Census—Slave Schedule** lists that Edmond Cook had 6 black slaves (female, 38; female, 22; male, 18; male, 5; male, 3; male, 1).

1860 US Federal Census—Slave Schedule.

55

The **1870 US Census** lists Edmund as a "farmer" and Mary Ann as "keeping house," with Mary A., age 21, "at home," and Thomas P., age 21, "farmer." They were living in Calloway County, Kentucky. Thomas was born in 1851, so he was probably 19 instead of 21.

1870 US Census.

Edmund died in 1872.

The **1880 US Census** lists Mary Ann, 65, "keeping house" with her daughter, H.H., age 30, "at home"; her son, Thos P., age 28, "lawyer"; and her daughter, M.A., age 24, "millner." They lived in Murray, Calloway County, Kentucky.

1880 US Census.

~~~

Elias Power Cook is the Cook family ancestor. See details in the Paternal Third Generation.

Summary of Paternal Third Generation

Elias Power Cook was born in Virginia as the sixth of twelve siblings. In his youth, he moved to Calloway County, Kentucky, which is just north across the state line of Henry County, Tennessee. In 1861, at age 19, he enlisted in the Tennessee Infantry as a private in the Confederate Army. He was wounded and "crippled" in battle. It's not known how long he served in the Army, but this unit surrendered in 1865.

His father, Edmund, died in 1872, when Elias was 30.

He married Sarah Elizabeth "Ballie" Milliken in 1877, when he was 35, in Henry County, Tennessee. They had 6 children in 11 years.

Their first child was born when Elias was 40. The last child was born when Elias was 51. Tera Monroe Cook (1882-1957), Rupert Berber (183-1961), Heber Amos Cook (1886-after 1919), Ruby Irma Cook Stover (1888-1975), Eric Power Cook (1890-1987), Gela Lela Cook (1893-1972).

He served in the 1891-1892 Tennessee Legislature.

His mother, Mary Ann, died in 1895, when Elias was 53.

Elias and Ballie moved with their children from Paris, Henry County, Tennessee, to Independence, Jackson County, Missouri, in 1905, according to their son Eric. However, Elias P. Cook's obituary said that the family "located at Independence in 1895." The **1900 US Census** showed the Cook family living in Tennessee.

The obituary lists him as a retired schoolteacher and farmer. He farmed until 1904, when he was 62.

Elias died at home from "lobar pneumonia" at the age of 77. He's buried in Mound Grove Cemetery (Independence, Missouri).

Gela Lela Cook is the Cook ancestor in the family line. See details in Summary of Maternal/Paternal Second Generation.

~~~

Elias Power Cook

Born 6 Apr 1842 (Virginia); died 12 May 1919 of lobar pneumonia at age 77. He "died at 9 o'clock Monday night at his home, 1028 West Maple Avenue, Independence." Buried in Mound Grove Cemetery (Independence, Missouri). His obituary lists him as a retired schoolteacher and farmer. Married Sarah Elizabeth "Ballie" Milliken (1859-1921) on 6 Dec 1877 (Henry County, Tennessee).

Elias Power Cook, Nashville, Tennessee, circa 1900s.

Elias Power Cook, Independence, Missouri, circa 1910s.

E. P. Cook and tomato plants at 1028 West Maple, Independence, Missouri, circa 1910s.

Elias Cook enlisted at the age of 19 (13 Nov 1861) at Union City, Tennessee, as a private, 33rd Regiment, Tennessee Infantry, Company C, Confederate Army. He fought in the battle of Shiloh. E.P. Cook later served in the 47th General Assembly of the Tennessee House of Representatives (1891-1892), no party affiliation listed.

Confederate Tennessee Troops, 33rd Regiment, Tennessee Infantry, Overview

"33rd Infantry Regiment was formed in October, 1861, near Union City, Tennessee. The men were recruited in the counties of Obion, Madison, Lake, Hardeman, and Weakley. Company C contained men from Calloway County, Kentucky. It fought at Shiloh and Perryville, then was stationed at Shelbyville for a few months. The unit served under Generals Stewart, Strahl, and Palmer, and in December, 1862, was consolidated with the 31st Regiment. It partcipated in many battles of the Army of Tennessee from Murfreesboro to Atlanta, moved back to Tennessee with Hood, and was active in North Carolina. This regiment lost 20 killed, 103 wounded, and 17 missing at Shiloh and reported 33 casualties at Perryville. The 31st/33rd lost twenty-three percent of the 379 engaged at Murfreesboro, then the 33rd had 24 disabled at Missionary Ridge and totalled 124 men and 69 arms in December, 1863. It surrendered in April, 1865. The field officers were Colonels Alexander W. Campbell, Warner P. Jones, and Robert N. Payne, and Lieutenant Colonel Henry C. McNeill."

—National Park Service, US Department of the Interior

"Elias P. Cook moved to Kentucky in his youth. He enlisted in the Confederate Army in 1860 and was wounded during a Civil War battle. He served in the Tennessee legislature from 1891 to 1892 and then farmed until 1904, despite being crippled from a battle wound. Elias was baptized and confirmed a member of the Reorganized Church of Jesus Christ of Latter Day Saints on 27 July (August) 1897 at Paris, Henry, Tennessee, by J. F. Henson. He was ordained a priest on 3 October (August) 1897 in Paris by T. W. Chatburn. He was ordained an elder in 1905. He attended the Foundry, Tennessee Branch and the Independence, Missouri Branch."

—Harvey B. Black, *Early Members of the Reorganized Church of Jesus Christ of Latter Day Saints*. Provo, Utah, 1996

E.P. Cook was listed as a male voter from Henry County, Tennessee, in 1891.

Enumeration of male voters, Henry County, Tennessee, 1891.

The **1900 US Census** lists Elias P.'s occupation as "farmer," and living with "Bally E." in Henry County, Tennessee. Six children were living at home, ages 18 to 7.

1900 US Census.

The **1910 US Census** lists Elias (retired) and Ballie living in Independence, Missouri, with their children Eric (20) and Gala [sic] (17). Also residing in the house were their son Berber (R.B.), who is listed as a "salesman," and his wife Grace.

> COOK—Elias P. Cook, 77 years old, a retired school teacher and farmer, died at 9 o'clock Monday night at his home, 1028 West Maple Avenue, Independence. He was born in Virginia. He located at Independence in 1895. Surviving him are his widow, Mrs. Dallie Cook; four sons, Tera M. and Eric P. Cook, both of Independence, R. B. Cook of Sibley, this county, and Heber A. Cook of Fulton, Ky., and two daughters, Mrs. Irma Stover and Miss Gela Cook, both of Independence. The funeral services will be held at 10:30 o'clock this morning at the Stone Church in Independence. Burial will be at Mound Grove Cemetery.

Elias Power Cook, 1842-1919, died age 77.

~~~

Summary of Elias and Ballie Cook Family

Elias (35) married Ballie (18) on 6 Dec 1877 (Henry County, Tennessee).

Tennessee record of marriage of E. P. Cook to Ballie Milliken, 6 Dec 1877.

They had 6 children in 11 years. Their first child was born when Elias was 40 and Ballie was 23. The last child was born when Elias was 51 and Ballie was 34.

Back: Heber and Ballie (mother). Front: Tera, Eric, E.P. (father) holding Gela, Berber, Irma, circa 1893.

1. Tera Monroe Cook (1882-1957). 2. Rupert Berber (1863-1961). 3. Heber Amos Cook (1886-after 1919).
4. Ruby Irma Cook Stover (1888-1975). 5. Eric Power Cook (1890-1987). 6. Gela Lela Cook Moorman (1893-1972). See details in Summary of Maternal/Paternal Second Generation.

**Left: Back: Myrtle (Tera's wife), Gela, Eric, Irma, Berber, Ballie (mother); front: Tera holding son Kenneth; Elias Power (E. P.) Cook (father); location unknown, date circa 1906.
Right: Elias P. and Ballie Cook, Mound Grove Cemetery, Independence, Missouri.**

~~~

Gela Moorman is the Cook family ancestor. See details in Summary of Maternal/Paternal Second Generation.

~~~

Summary of Maternal/Paternal Second Generation

Kentucky school classes: Gela (second row, second from left), Eric (second row, third from left), Tera, Irma, Heber or Berber (top row, three tallest children in the middle), circa 1905.

Tera Monroe Cook

Born 2 Jan 1882 (Obion County, Tennessee); died 20 Aug 1957 of "coronary occlusion" (also had diabetes) at age 75 (Independence, Missouri). Buried at Mound Grove Cemetery (Independence, Missouri). Married Myrtle Mae Farrow (1887-1957) on 29 Nov 1905 (Jackson County, Missouri). Tera and Myrtle had 1 child: **Kenneth Harold Cook** (1906-1966).

According to Virginia Dungan, her uncle and aunt (Tera and Myrtle) owned a roller skating rink in Maywood (listed as "The Wings" in the 1936 Independence city directory, located at 10314 Van Horn Road, Independence, Missouri). Virginia's daughter, Joni, remembers skating at a rink at 733 S. Northern Blvd., Independence, Missouri, in the 1960s that was owned by Tera and Myrtle.

Addresses for Tera and Myrtle Cook

- 1910—1428 W. Maple, Independence, Missouri.
- 1918—120 S. Crysler, Independence.
- 1924—1320 W. Maple, Independence, listed as "cab mkr" [cabinet maker].
- 1930-1932—1322 W. Maple, Independence, listed as "carp" [carpenter] and Myrtle was listed as "clk [clerk] Drown & Farrow."
- 1935—10111 Van Horn (later renamed Truman Road), Independence.
- 1936—10201 Van Horn Road, Independence. Myrtle listed at "The Wings" roller skating located at 10314 Van Horn Road. Kenneth was listed as "floor mgr The Wings."
- 1938-1942—10111 Van Horn Road, Independence. Kenneth did not appear in the Independence city directory after 1940.
- 1957—808 W. Maple, Independence.

Tera Monroe Cook, World War 2 draft registration card, 1942. He was 60 years old.

Myrtle died in March 1957 from "hypertensive arteriosclerotic cardiovascular disease with uremia." She also had diabetes. On Myrtle's death certificate she's listed as "Male," and the informant was Katherine Farrow, her sister-in-law. Her street address is listed as 1041 W. Truman, two blocks west of the 808 West Maple Avenue house where Tera was listed as living.

Tera died at home five months later in August 1957 from "coronary occlusion, sudden death." He also had diabetes. The informant was Kenneth Cook, Hutchinson, Kansas.

Tera M. Cook died age 75 and spouse Myrtle M. Cook died age 69, Mound Grove Cemetery, Independence, Missouri.

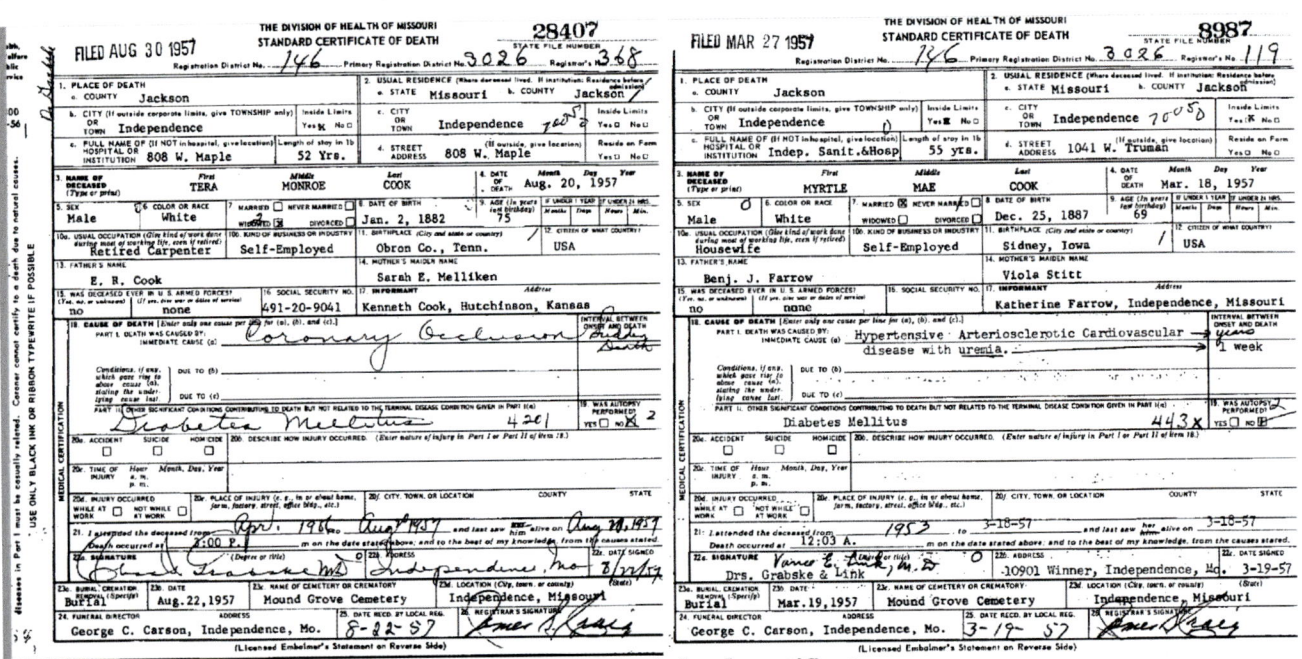

Tera and Myrtle Cook death certificates.

~~~

Kenneth Harold Cook (1906-1966). In 1940, at age 33, Kenneth was living with his parents in Independence, Missouri. In April 1943, Kenneth married Nancy M. Broadhead (1913-1969). They had 1 child Mary E. Cook (~1944-after 1969). During World War 2, he served as a captain in the US Army Signal Corps. He was in charge of a vital radio transmitter that linked Paris to New York. Kenneth belonged to the Rotary Club and was also a Shriner. He was a member of Trinity Methodist Church in Hutchinson, Kansas. In a 1953 county census, Kenneth (54), Nancy (47), and Mary (13) lived in Hutchinson, Kansas. In a 1962 city directory, Kenneth was listed as "chief eng KTVH." KTVH was a CBS affiliate station in Hutchinson, Kansas, which operated from 1953 until 1983 when the call letters were changed to KWCH. Kenneth died unexpectedly at age 59. Kenneth and Nancy are buried in Saint Joseph, Missouri.

Kenneth Harold Cook, Mount Mora Cemetery, Saint Joseph, Missouri, died age 59.

~~~

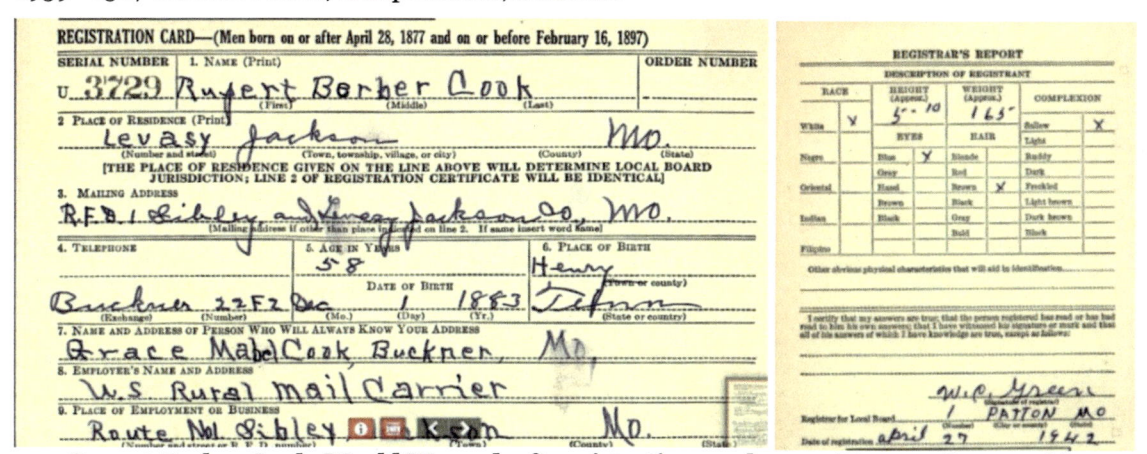

Rupert Berber Cook

Born 1 Dec 1883 (Paris, Tennessee); died 9 Mar 1961 of "carcinoma of head of pancreas and pulmonary edema" (also had diabetes) at age 77 (Independence, Missouri). Buried Mound Grove Cemetery (Independence, Missouri). Married Grace Mabel Shupe (1889-1965) on 3 Aug 1909 (Henry County, Tennessee). They had 6 children: ***Raymond Berber "R.B." Cook*** (1910-1965), ***Ardyce May Cook Banker*** (1912-1992), ***Scott Elias Cook*** (1914-2001), ***Leota Lucille Cook Pigg*** (1916-1986), ***Joseph Doyle Cook*** (1923-2008), ***Betty Lavelle Cook Ballmer*** (1929-2004).

Addresses for Berber and Grace Cook

- 1900—Henry County, Tennessee.
- 1910—725 W. Maple, Independence, Missouri.
- 1918—Sibley, Missouri.
- 1930-1940—Highway 24, Fort Osage, Missouri.
- 1942—Levasy, Missouri. His occupation was "US rural mail carrier." Virginia's notes state that they "raised watermelons."
- 1959—1507 Northern Blvd., Independence, Missouri.

Rupert Berber Cook, World War 2 draft registration card, 1942. He was 58 years old.

Berber died in 1961 at home of "carcinoma of head of pancreas" and "pulmonary edema—acute." He also had diabetes. His wife Grace died in 1965 of "cerebral thrombosis, generalized athero-sclerosis and arterial hypertension." She also had arteriosclerotic heart disease. The informant on Grace's death certificate was "Mrs. Charles Banker," her daughter Ardyce.

R. Berber Cook died age 77 and spouse Grace M. Cook died age 75, Mound Grove Cemetery, Independence, Missouri.

Berber and Grace Cook death certificates.

Grace Cook with Leota, Irma Cook Stover with Pearl, Altha Cook with Donald, circa 1916.

~~~

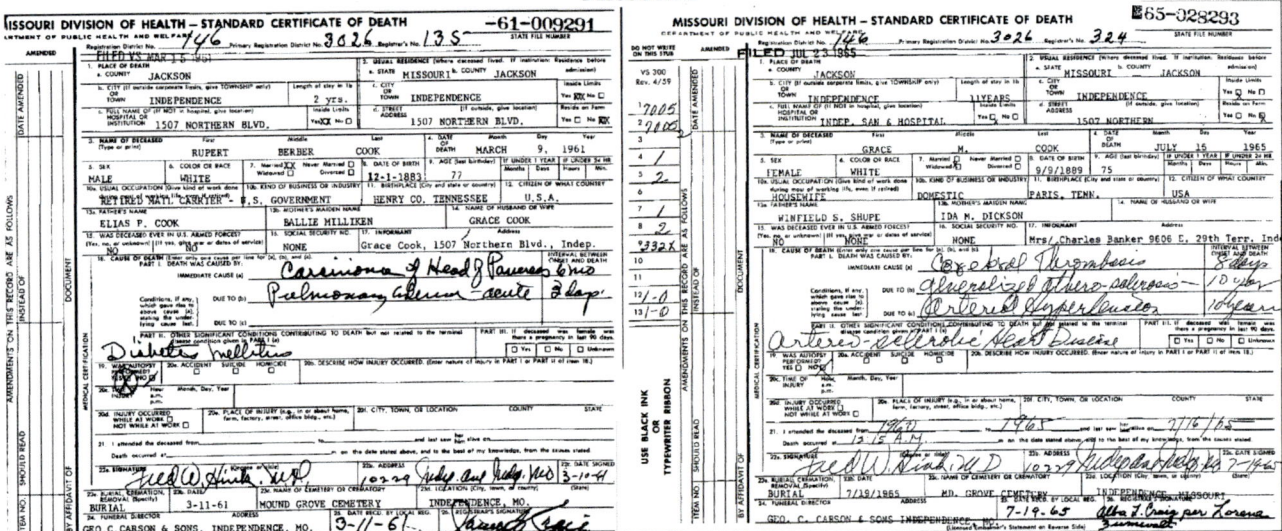

1. Raymond Berber "R.B." Cook (1910-1965) married Leona Louise Stoenner (1922-2005) on 5 Oct 1952 (Independence, Missouri). Virginia states they "lived next door to 1028." R.B. died of "coronary arteriosclerosis" at age 54. He and Leona are buried at Mound Grove Cemetery.

R.B. Cook's World War 2 draft registration card, 1940. He was 30.

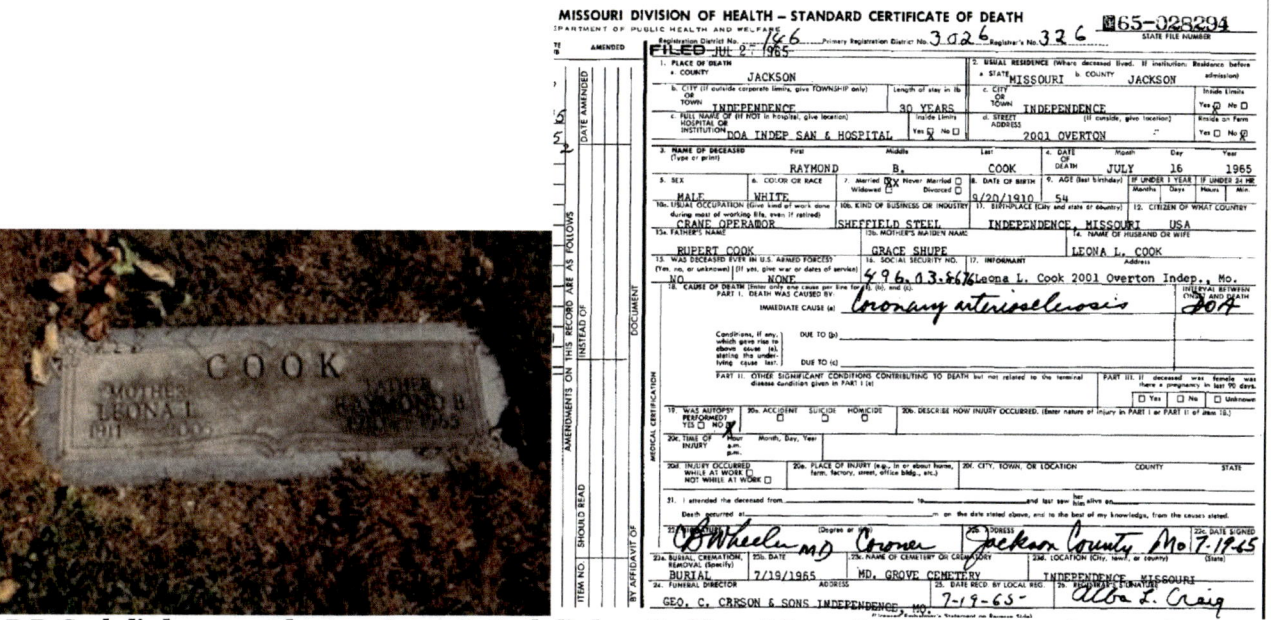

R.B. Cook died age 55 and spouse Leona L. Cook died age 83, Mound Grove Cemetery, Independence, Missouri.

2. Ardyce May Cook Banker (1912-1992) married Charles T. Banker (1914-1999) on 19 Jul 1947 (Independence, Missouri). They are buried at Mound Grove Cemetery.

Ardyce May Cook Banker died age 80 and spouse Charles Banker died age 85, Mound Grove Cemetery, Independence, Missouri.

3. Scott Elias Cook (1914-2001) married Zelma Lee McKendry (1916-1992) in 1936 (Missouri). They had 2 children: Thomas Scott Cook (1937-1951), Patricia Ann Cook Smith (1942-2014). Thomas died at age 13 from "bulbar poliomyelitis." Scott was a Masonic member, a farmer, and a salesman. Scott and Zelma and Thomas are buried at Mound Grove Cemetery.

Scott Cook died age 87 and spouse Zelma Lee Cook died age 76 and son Thomas S. Cook died age 13, Mound Grove Cemetery, Independence, Missouri. Right: daughter Pat Smith.

4. Leota Lucille Cook Pigg (1916-1986) married Joseph Arthur Pigg (1914-1992) on 28 May 1936 (Kansas City, Missouri). They had 2 children: Sylvia A. (1938-alive 2021) and Gary B.(1939-alive 2021). Leota and Joseph are buried at Oak Grove Cemetery, Missouri.

Leota Cook Pigg died age 70 and Joseph Pigg died age 78, Oak Grove Cemetery, Missouri.

5. Joseph Doyle Cook (1923-2008). Joseph and Norma Jean Race (1923/1924-2002) had a premature son who lived one day (18 Apr 1944-19 Apr 1944)—see death certificate on next page. About 1946, Joseph married Mary Margaret Roark (1926-2010). They had one son Robert Doyle Cook (1947-2004) and one daughter (no information). Joseph served in the US Army Air Forces during World War 2. Joseph and Mary are buried in Riverside National Cemetery, California.

Left: Infant son died 18 Apr 1944, Salem Church Cemetery, Independence, Missouri.
Right: Joseph Doyle Cook died age 85, Riverside National Cemetery, California.

6. Betty Lavelle Cook Ballmer (1929-2004) married Dallas Eldon Ballmer (1927-2006) on 31 Dec 1949 (Independence, Missouri). They had 6 children: Vicki Harvey, Lisa Libich, Lori Luther, Scotti Pittman, Steve Ballmer, Dallas J. Ballmer. Betty and Dallas died in Denham Springs, Louisiana. Unknown burial details.

Betty Lavelle Cook Ballmer and spouse Dallas Eldon Ballmer.

~~~

Heber Amos Cook

Born 23 Mar 1886 (Paris, Tennessee). Unknown death date. Last known correspondence was in Aug 1919 and last mention was in May 1919. Unknown burial location. In the **1900 US Census,** Heber was listed in Paris, Tennessee, 14 years old. The Cook family moved from Tennessee to Missouri in 1905. Unable to locate Heber in the 1910 US Census and beyond. Heber (27) married Emma Pearl McClain (1882-1954) Boaz (32) on 19 Jan 1914 (Jackson County, Missouri). (Emma had been a widow for 3½ years.) By 1926, Heber and Emma were divorced with no known children.

Heber A. Cook and Emma P. [McClain] Boaz marriage license, Jackson County, Missouri.
Note that Guy D. Cook, Emma's brother-in-law, signed the affidavit.

Of interest is that Heber's wife Emma McClain's older sister, Luella "Ella" Frances McClain (1873-1951) married Elisha William Stover (1872-1919) in 1901 (Obion, Tennessee). Elisha was an older brother to James Walter Stover (1881-1953) who married Heber's sister, Ruby Irma Cook (1888-1975) in 1908 (Independence, Missouri). Thank you to Gayle Brooks for this information.

~~~

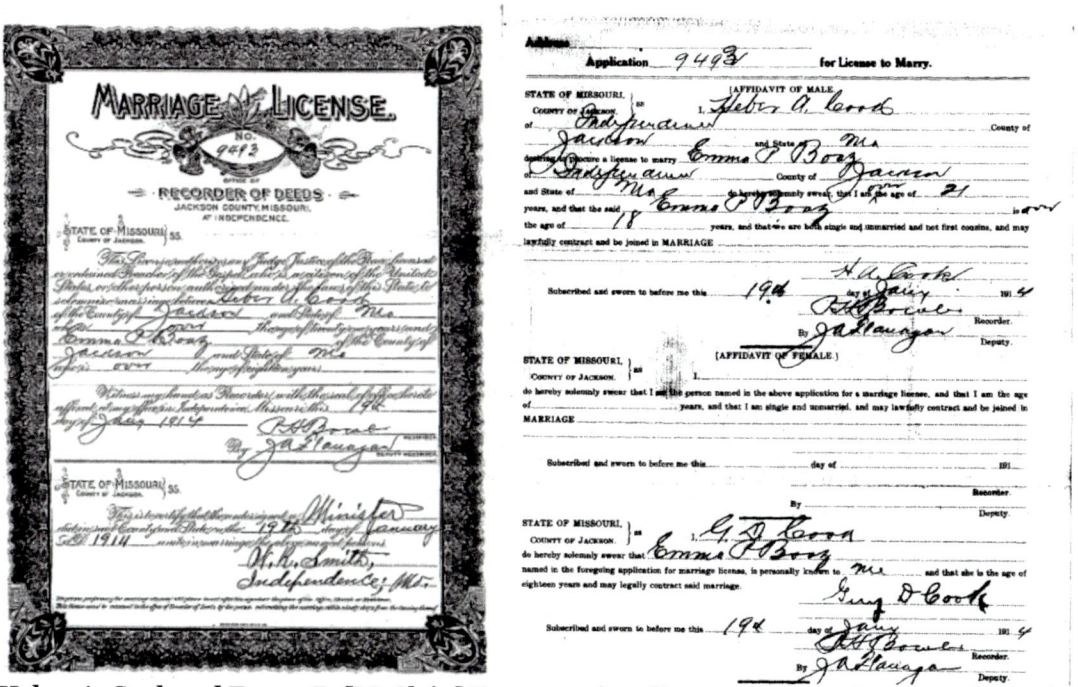

Emma McClain (1882-1954) was first married to John David Boaz (1873-1910). A dual headstone is in the Boaz Cemetery in Hickman, Kentucky, although Emma is buried in Independence, Missouri. J. D. was first married in July 1896 (Graves, Kentucky) to Eula Mae Pullen (1878-1897), but she died nine months later in March 1897 at age 18. J. D. married Emma on 3 Sep 1906, unknown location, but probably Kentucky. They were married until J. D. died in 1910 in Hickman, Kentucky, at age 36.

In the **1910 US Census,** Emma Boaz (27) is listed as wife of J. D. Boaz (36), and they had been married for 4 years. They lived in Hickman, Kentucky, on a farm that they owned. J. D. is listed as a farmer. No children.

Heber and Emma married in 1914 in Missouri. In a letter written in the 1970s by Heber's sister, Gela wrote, "Blair McClain was the son of J. R. [James Robert, 1868-1941] McClain whose sister Emma married your Uncle Heber and [his sister] Gertie [Gertrude May McClain, 1885-1957] married my cousin Guy [David Cook, 1884-1986] . . . J. R. McClain [was one] of our loved preachers living in Fulton, Kentucky."

On the 1918 draft card, Heber and Emma's permanent address is 1028 W. Maple, Independence, Missouri, Heber's parents' home. He was listed as 32 and his occupation was carpenter. The card lists his employer as "King Lumber Company," in Quantico, Prince William County, Virginia. However, a search for businesses from 1805-1955 in that area turned up nothing with that name. There was a King Lumber Company in Charlottesville, Albemarle County, Virginia, about 90 miles away. It was out of business by the 1930s, largely due to the Great Depression. It could be that Heber, a carpenter, was working on a job in Quantico, Virginia, for King Lumber. The draft card has Local Board addresses for Manassas, Virginia, and also for Independence, Missouri.

Heber Amos Cook, World War 1 draft registration card, 1918. He was 32. The card lists Heber as tall, stout, gray hair, brown eyes, and "nothing lost" in reference to physical limitations.

In August 1918, Heber sent a postcard to his mother.

Postmark: Washington, D.C., Aug 22, 1918, 1 PM; 2 cent stamp

To: Mrs. E. P. Cook, 1028 W Maple, Independence, Mo

Arrived Here OK. Leave here at 2 PM. Will write soon.

Lovingly, H.A.C [Heber Amos Cook, Ballie's 32-year-old son]

~~~

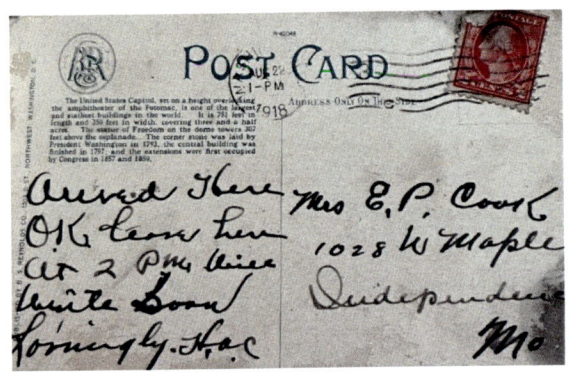

In May 1919, the *KC Star* obituary for Heber's father states he was in Fulton, Kentucky, about 45 miles from his hometown of Paris, Tennessee. It's not known what he was doing and if Emma was with him. Many of the Cook family relatives still lived in the Kentucky/Tennessee area.

COOK—Elias P. Cook, 77 years old, a retired school teacher and farmer, died at 9 o'clock Monday night at his home, 1028 West Maple Avenue, Independence. He was born in Virginia. He located at Independence in 1895. Surviving him are his widow, Mrs. Dallie Cook; four sons, Tera M. and Eric P. Cook, both of Independence, R B. Cook of Sibley, this county, and Heber A. Cook of Fulton, Ky., and two daughters, Mrs. Irma Stover and Miss Gela Cook, both of Independence. The funeral services will be held at 10:30 o'clock this morning at the Stone Church in Independence. Burial will be at Mound Grove Cemetery.

Later that year, in a letter dated November 1919, Jennie Hays asks her sister Ballie Cook (Heber's mother), "Has Heba [sic] moved out there yet" in the same sentence that she mentions Ballie's other children (Irma, Gela, Tera, Berber, and Eric), which might indicate that Heber (and possibly Emma) were moving to Missouri from Fulton, Kentucky. Emma's obituary indicates she moved to Independence, Missouri, about 1922. In 1926, Emma (but not Heber) was listed in the Independence city directory.

According to Heber's niece Virginia Dungan, Aunt Emma "wanted to squeeze me—but I didn't want her to break my bones." Virginia was born in 1920, so if she remembers Aunt Emma hugging her, it was probably during the 1920s in Missouri, before Virginia moved to New Jersey in 1927. Virginia indicated that Heber left Emma and was not heard from again. There was some mystery in the family about this.

It's unknown when and where Emma and Heber divorced, but it was before 1926. In the 1926 Independence city directory, Emma McClain is listed at the Palace Café, 316 S. Grand, working with her older sister, Martha Jane McClain (1867-1936), a kitchen helper. Heber is not listed in the city directory as a resident of Independence.

~~~

Ruby Irma Cook Stover

Born 22 Jun 1888 (Whitlock, Tennessee); died 14 May 1975 at age 86 (Independence, Missouri). Married James Walter Stover (1881-1953) on 1 Jan 1908 (Independence, Missouri). Walter died of a coronary thrombosis and hypertension at age 71 "in his summer cabin in the Ozarks" [Camden, Missouri]. Irma and Walter are buried at Mound Grove Cemetery (Independence, Missouri). They had 5 children: ***Clyde Walter Stover*** (1908-1979), ***Ruby Emma Stover Willoughby*** (1911-1928), ***Mildred Louise Stover Van Artsdalen*** (1912-1969), ***Gela Pearl Stover Stevenson*** (1916-2011), ***Mary Elaine Stover Resch*** (1925-1995).

Ballie with daughter Irma, circa 1889.

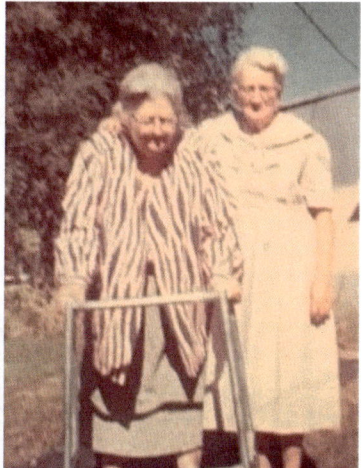

Left and middle: Irma Cook Stover. Right: sisters Gela Cook Moorman and Irma, circa 1970s.

Addresses for Walter and Irma Cook Stover

- 1910—731 West South Avenue, Independence, Missouri.
- 1920–1948—1312 West Kensington, Independence, Missouri.

The **1910 US Census** lists Walter (grocery storekeeper) and "Erma" at 731 West South Avenue (Independence, Missouri) with Clyde W., 1, and Walter's sister, Jessie C., single, 23 (seamstress).

1910 US Census.

The **1920 US Census** lists James W. (laborer, oil refinery) and Ruby I. at 1312 W. Kensington (Independence, Missouri) with Clyde W., 10; Ruby E., 8; Mildred L., 7; Gela P., 3.

1920 US Census.

The **1930 US Census** lists James W. (brick mason, oil refinery) and Irma R. at 1312 W. Kensington (Independence, Missouri) with Pearl G., 13; Elaine M., 4; along with daughter Mildred and son-in-law Russell VanArtsdalen and grandson James W., 1.

1930 US Census.

The **1940 US Census** lists James W. (brick mason, oil refinery) and Irma R. at 1312 W. Kensington (Independence, Missouri) with Elaine, 14.

DIES AT A SUMMER HOME.

Heart Attack Apparently Suffered by James W. Stover, 71.

James Walter Stover, 71, of 1312 Kensington avenue, Independence, died yesterday in a summer cabin on the Lake of the Ozarks twenty-six miles south of Versailles, apparently of a heart attack.

Mr. Stover and his wife, Mrs. Ruby Irma Stover, had gone to the cabin Monday for the summer.

Mr. Stover was born in Arkansas and moved to Independence forty-seven years ago from Fulton County, Kentucky. He retired in 1945 after twenty-eight years as a brick mason at the Standard Oil company refinery at Sugar Creek. Previously he was a grocer in Independence. Mr. Stover was a member of the Stone church, Reorganized Latter Day Saints.

Besides his wife, he is survived by a son, Clyde W. Stover, 2708 Englewood terrace, Independence; three daughters, Mrs. Mildred Van Artsdalen, 113 North Crescent avenue, Fairmount; Mrs. Pearl Stevenson, 811 Devon avenue, Independence, and Mrs. Elaine Resch, 1208 North Main street, Independence; and two sisters, Mrs. Sophie Hemphill of the home, and Mrs. Jessie Denny, 7912 Ward parkway.

Walter Stover death certificate and *KC Star* article, 13 Jun 1953.

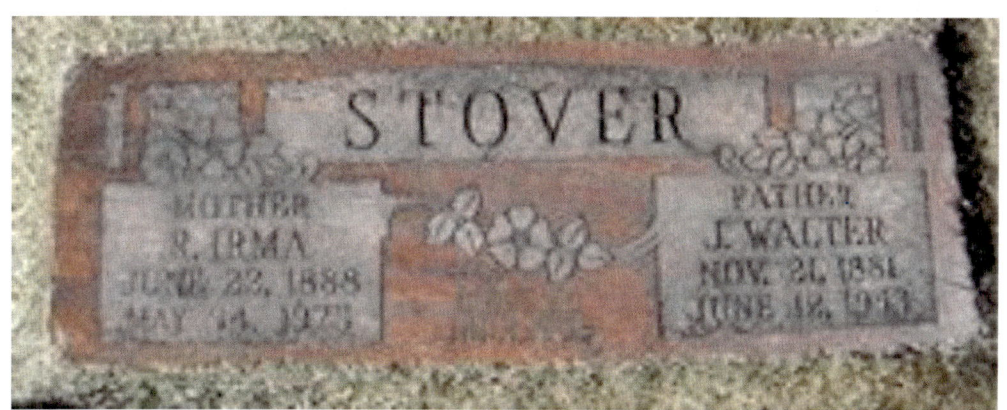

Irma Cook Stover died age 86 and spouse Walter Stover died age 71, Mound Grove Cemetery, Independence, Missouri.

Stover family, Walter (seated), Russell Van Artsdalen and spouse Mildred, Clyde and spouse Muriel, unknown man, Irma (seated), and Pearl. Jim Van Artsdalen sitting in rocker, Elaine standing in front, circa 1928.

~~~

1. Clyde Walter Stover (1908-1979) and Muriel Kirk Stover (1908-1996) were married 16 Feb 1919. They had 3 children: Shirley Louise Stover Winkinhofer (1936-2014), Betty Jeanne Stover (1939-1981), Robert "Bob" Kirk Stover (1946-2012). They owned a lakeside cabin at Sunrise Beach, Missouri, near Oscar Moorman's cabin. Clyde and Muriel are buried at Floral Hills Cemetery, Kansas City, Missouri.

Clyde Walter Stover World War 2 draft registration card, 1940. He was 31.

Left to right: Muriel Kirk Stover (Clyde's wife), son Bob Stover, daughter Shirley Stover Winkinhofer, Clyde Stover, daughter Betty Stover. Courtesy Sherry Winkinhofer, married to Kenneth Winkinhofer, Shirley's stepson.

CLYDE W. STOVER

Clyde Walter Stover, 70, of Sunrise Beach, Mo., died Wednesday at the Lake of the Ozarks General Hospital. He was born in Independence and lived most of his life in this area before moving to Sunrise Beach in 1977. He was a retired carpenter and electrician. He was a member of the RLDS Church and was God and country director for the RLDS Center. He was a member of the Mic-O-Say scout organization. He leaves his wife, Muriel K. Stover, of the home; a son, Robert K. Stover, Sunrise Beach; two daughters, Mrs. Shirley Winkenhofer, Kansas City, and Miss Betty Stover, Independence; and two sisters, Mrs. Pearl Stevenson and Mrs. Elaine Resh, both of Independence. Services will be at 11 a.m. Saturday at Speaks Chapel, Independence; burial in Floral Hills Cemetery. Friends may call from 7 to 9 p.m. Friday at the chapel. The family suggests contributions to the Rehabilitation Institute of Kansas City, 3011 Baltimore.

Left: Clyde and spouse Muriel Stover, December 1971. Right: *KC Star* article, 13 Dec 1979.

Shirley Louise Stover (1936-2014) married George William Winkinhofer (1924-2010) on 19 Nov 1966 (Jackson County, Missouri). George had 2 children, Shirley's stepchildren: Kenneth Gene (1952-2012) and Sherry (after 1952-alive 2021). Shirley and George are buried at Oak Ridge Memory Gardens (Independence, Missouri).

> Shirley S. Winkinhofer, 77, Independence, MO passed away Feb. 1, 2014 . . . In lieu of flowers the family requests contributions to the Alzheimer's Association . . . Shirley was born Nov. 1, 1936 in Independence, MO and graduated from Central High School. She worked at Armco Steel for twenty-eight years before retiring in 1985. She was best known for her ceramics shop, Wink's Ceramics, which she owned and operated from her home for over forty years. She taught ceramics classes and served as a judge at many competitions. She was a member of the Ceramics Guild and Community of Christ Good Shepherd Congregation. She was also a painter and gardener. Shirley was preceded in death by her husband George Winkinhofer, son Kenneth Winkinhofer, sister Betty Stover and brother Robert Stover. She is survived by daughter Sherry Winkinhofer; granddaughter Elizabeth Winkinhofer, both of Smithville, MO; cousins Viola Berry; John Stevenson; Jim Resch, all of Blue Springs, MO; Jan Jones; and Pat Cook both of Independence, MO.

Betty Jeanne Stover (1939-1981). Died age 42. No known spouse or children. Unknown burial location.

Robert "Bob" Kirk Stover (1946-2012). Died age 66. No known spouse or children. He was cremated.

> Robert (Bob) Kirk Stover 66 years of age passed away Sunday, October 21, 2012 at St. Luke's Hospital in Kansas City, MO. He was born January 18, 1946 in Independence, MO. His parents, Clyde Walter Stover and Muriel (Kirk) Stover, and sister, Betty Jeanne Stover preceded him in death. He is survived by his sister, Shirley Louise (Stover) Winkinhofer, niece, Sherry Winkinhofer, and numerous cousins.
>
> He graduated from Van Horn High School in 1964, and attended the University of Michigan. He worked with his father in the cabinet building and electrical businesses prior to moving to the Lake of the Ozarks. After moving he worked as a carpenter before gaining employment with the Postal Service where he worked as a mail carrier until he retired.
>
> Bob loved watching the wildlife around his property and carried dog biscuits on his mail route for all of the dogs that would meet him at the mail box. Bob was a member of the MOM Black Powder Club, and members held the monthly target practices at his shooting range. He also allowed members to engage in bow hunting on his property.
>
> Memorial services for Bob will be held at . . . Corner Stone Community of Christ Church, 1316 S. Osage, Independence, MO. In lieu of flowers, contributions in memory of Bob may be made to the American Heart Association, or the Diabetic Foundation, or charity of choice.

~~~

2. Ruby Emma Stover Willoughby was born on 15 Jan 1911. She was 17 when she married Ammon H. Willoughby (1908-1966) about 1927. She died in childbirth on 10 Feb 1928. Their son, Paul Willoughby, died 10 Feb 1928. Emma's death certificate is shown below. No death certificate was found for Paul. Ammon later married Mildred A. Wilcox and had two sons with her.

Walter and Irma's daughter, Emma, 1911-1928, died age 17, of anemia related to pregnancy. Emma is buried in Mound Grove Cemetery, Independence, Missouri. The Mound Grove Cemetery records indicate that her son Paul Willoughby is also buried there. He was "0" days old. "No Marker—perhaps buried with mother, Ruby Emma, who died same date."

~~~

3. *Mildred Louise Stover Van Artsdalen* (1912-1969) married Russell Victor Van Artsdalen (1906-1981) on 14 Jan 1928. They had 3 children: James William Van Artsdalen (1928-2019), Margaret Louise Van Artsdalen Flippin (1930-2018), Helen Francis Van Artsdalen Fitzwater (1933-2003). Mildred died at age 56 due to cancer of the liver and pancreas. Mildred and Russell are buried at Mount Washington Cemetery, Independence, Missouri.

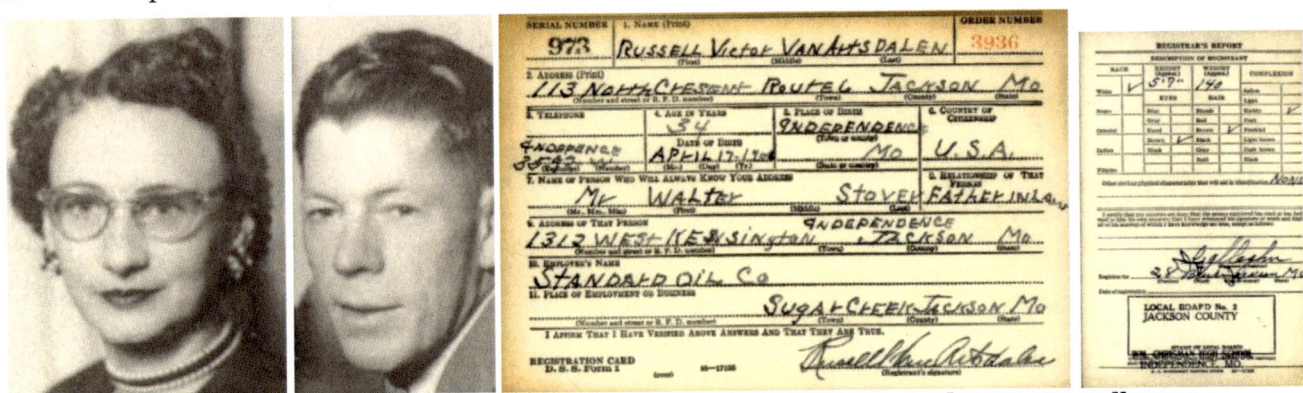

Mildred and Russell Van Artsdalen. World War 2 draft registration card, 1942. Russell was 34.

Mildred Van Artsdalen death certificate.

James William Van Artsdalen (1928-2019) married Winola Hart Van Artsdalen (~1936-after 2020) on 14 Feb 1959. James served in Korea as a US Air Force T/Sgt. He's buried in the Central Texas State Veterans Cemetery, Killeen, Texas. They had 2 children: James Van Artsdalen and John Van Artsdalen.

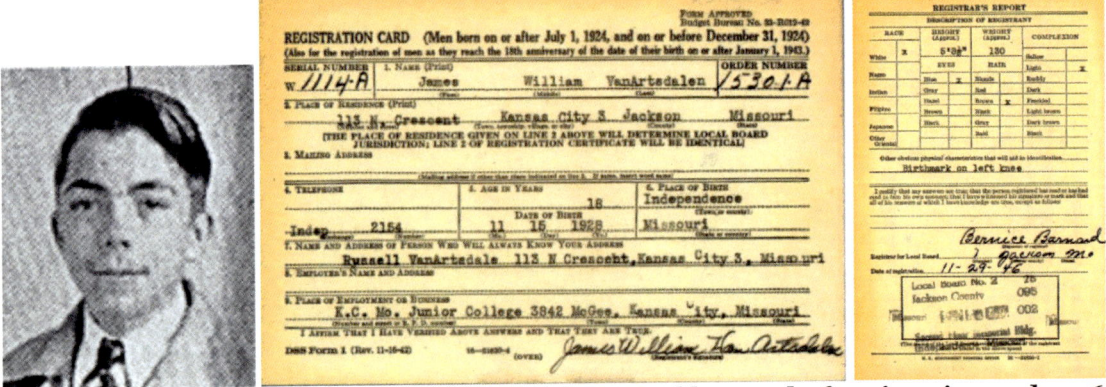

James Van Artsdalen, Northeast High School yearbook, 1944. World War 2 draft registration card, 1946, age 18.

Margaret Louise Van Artsdalen Flippin (1930-2018) married Herbert Lawrence Flippin (1929-2006) on 14 Jan 1949. They had 4 children: Connie Flippin Kincaid, Larry Flippin, Brian Flippin, Bruce Flippin. Margaret's body was donated to medical science—the Nebraska Anatomical Board.

Helen Francis Van Artsdalen Fitzwater (1933-2003) married Marvin Edward Fitzwater (1931-1988) on 24 Feb 1950. They had 6 children: Frances "Frannie" Fitzwater Grubb, Eddie Fitzwater (1952-2011), Cheryl Fitzwater Garringer, Gary Fitzwater, Michelle Fitzwater O'Guin, and Denise Fitzwater Pace. Helen and Marvin are buried at Mount Washington Cemetery, Independence, Missouri.

4. Gela Pearl Stover Stevenson (1916-2011) married John William "Bill" Stevenson (1912-1972) on 5 Jun 1936 (Independence, Missouri). They had 2 children: Viola Stevenson and John Stevenson Jr. Pearl and Bill are buried in Mound Grove Cemetery, Independence, Missouri.

Left: Pearl standing in front of Irma, Walter holding Elaine, circa 1926.
Right: Virginia Dungan and Pearl Stevenson, Gulf Breeze, Florida, Jul 1978.

Pearl Stevenson, 94, of Blue Springs, MO, died January 2, 2011. She was a life long resident of the Independence/Blue Springs area and a long time member of Gudgell Park RLDS/Community of Christ Congregation. She is survived by her two children, Viola Berry and Johnny Stevenson; two grandsons, George Ressler and Ashley Stevenson; two great granddaughters, Misty Ressler and Melody Ressler; four great- great grandchildren; as well as many other loving family members.

Pearl Stevenson died age 94 and spouse Bill Stevenson died age 60, Mound Grove Cemetery, Independence, Missouri.

Viola P. Stevenson Berry Ressler (1938-2011).

Viola Stevenson, William Chrisman High School yearbook photos, 1954 and 1956.

John "Johnny" William Stevenson Jr. (1947-2011) married Joan. They had 1 child.

~~~

5. Mary Elaine Stover Resch (1925-1995) married Clarence Albert "Bud" Resch Jr. (1924-2009) on 15 Mar 1946 (Independence, Missouri). They had 3 children: Jim Resch, Janice Resch Jones, Pat Resch Cook. Elaine and Bud are buried at Mound Grove Cemetery.

Left: Elaine Stover, William Chrisman High School, 1943. Middle: Elaine and Bud Resch, unknown date. Right: Bud and Elaine Resch, March 1946.

Left: Elaine and Irma Stover. Middle: Irma Stover and Elaine Resch. Right: sisters Elaine (left) and Pearl Stover, unknown locations and dates.

Elaine Stover Resch died age 70 and spouse Bud Resch died age 84.

"Clarence A. "Bud" Resch, Jr., 84, Independence, MO passed away Feb. 28, 2009 . . . Bud was born Sept. 14, 1924 in Independence, MO and was a lifelong resident. He worked at TWA for thirty-one years and retired in 1986. After retirement, he worked at Schmitt Music in Independence. He was an Army Air Corps veteran of WW II and an Air Force veteran of the Korean Era. Bud was a member of the Community of Christ Church College Park Congregation, where he was a Priest and then an Elder. Utilizing his expertise in technology, he took it upon himself to record each week's sermon, transpose the recordings to cassette tapes and distribute them to people who were shut-ins so they could hear the message. He was also a member of the Independence Amateur Radio Club and was involved with the Boy Scouts of America in years past. He is survived by his son Jim Resch and wife Vicki, Blue Springs, MO; daughters Jan Jones and husband Dale, Summerville, SC; Pat Cook, Lee's Summit, MO; grandchildren Debbie Grainger and husband Jimmy, Independence, MO; Paxton Taylor and wife Angela, Lee's Summit, MO; Chris Resch, Lake Lotawana, MO; Jennie Jones and husband James, Portland, OR; Jeremy Cook, Warrensburg, MO; and six great-grandchildren."

Jim Resch (1949-alive 2021) married Vicki Jones. **Janice E. Resch** (1951-alive 2021) married Dale Alan Jones (1951-2018) 12 Aug 1972. Jan and Dale had a daughter: Jennifer. **Patricia May Resch** (1953-alive 2021) married (1) Gary L. Taylor (1952-?) on 18 Jun 1971 (Missouri). Patricia married (2) John M. Cook (1953-?) on 25 May 1977.

~~~

Eric Power Cook

Born 28 Feb 1890 (Paris, Tennessee); died 25 Feb 1987 at age 96 (Independence, Missouri). Buried Mound Grove Cemetery (Independence, Missouri). Married Ellen Altha Crick (1891-1965) on 21 Aug 1912. Altha's parents were born in Canada. Altha was born in Missouri. Eric and Altha had 2 children. **Donald William** (1916-1964) married Dorothy Adelyn Lanphear (1916-2005) on 8 Nov 1937 and **Margaret Louise "Peggy"** (1918-2003).

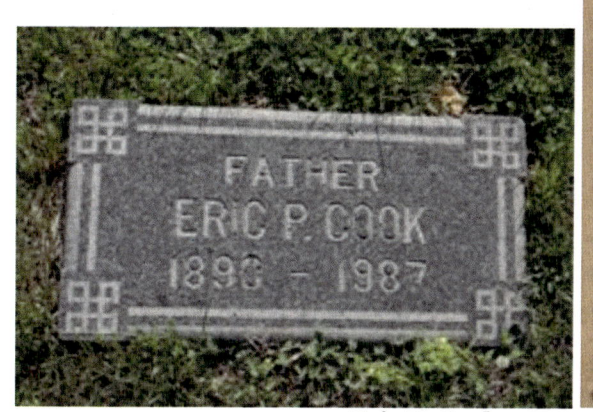

ERIC P. COOK

Eric P. Cook, 96, died Feb. 25, 1987, in the Resthaven Retirement Home, 1500 W. Truman Road, Independence, where he lived. He was born in Tennessee and lived in this area most of his life. Mr. Cook worked for the Independence Stove & Furnace Co. for 42 years and retired as secretary-treasurer in 1955. He was a member and elder of the Stone Church congregation of the Reorganized Church of Jesus Christ of Latter Day Saints. Survivors include a daughter, Margaret L. Cook, Independence. Services will be at 10 a.m. Friday at the Speaks Midtown Chapel; burial in Mound Grove Cemetery. Friends may call from 7 to 8:30 p.m. today at the chapel.

Eric P. Cook, 1890-1987, died age 96.

Addresses for Eric and Altha Cook

- 1910—1028 W. Maple, Independence, Missouri.
- 1920-1924—205 S. Pendleton, Independence. Listed "bkpr Indep Stove & Furnace Co."
- 1930-1942—1400 W. Short, listed as "sec Independence Stove & Furnace Co." telephone Indep 1186.

The **1920 US Census** lists Eric P. (bookkeeper) with Altha E. living at 205 South Pendleton Avenue with Donald, 3, and Margaret L., 1.

The **1930 US Census** lists Eric P. (secretary) with Ellen A. living at 1400 West Short with Donald W., 13, and Margaret L., 11.

The **1940 US Census** lists Eric (treasurer) with Althea living at 1400 West Short with Margaret, 21.

Left: Eric P. Cook, unknown date. Right: Altha with Don and Peggy, unknown date.

1. Donald William Cook (1916-1964). Died age 47 from acute coronary occlusion and coronary arteriosclerosis. He also had essential hypertension and exogenous obesity. Buried Mound Grove Cemetery. Married Dorothy Adelyn Lanphear (1916-2005) on 8 Nov 1937.

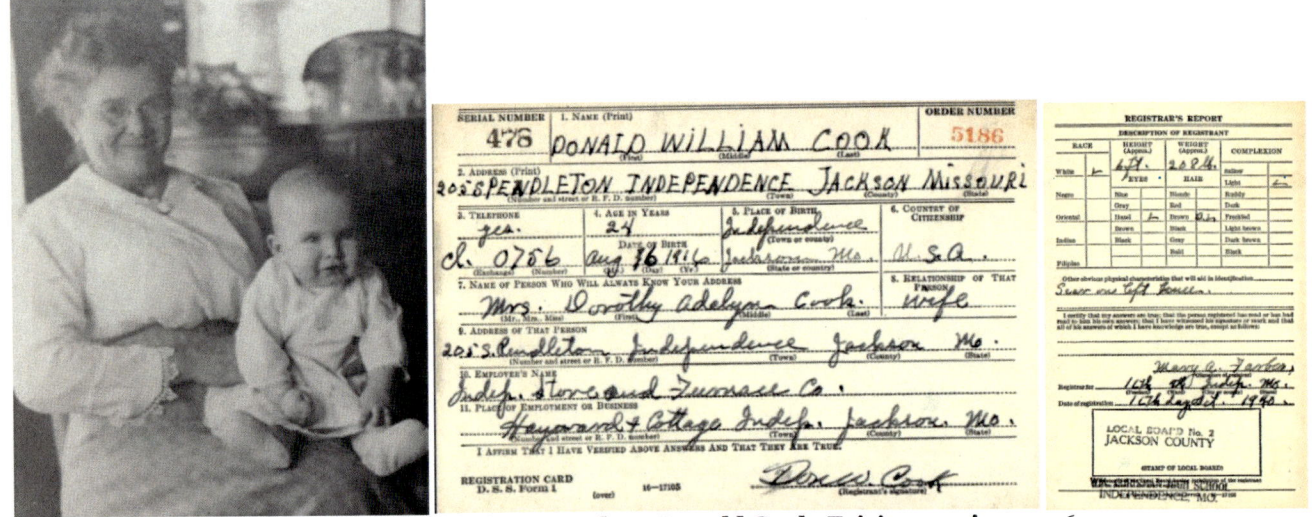

Left: Ballie Cook holding grandson Donald Cook, Eric's son, circa 1916.
Right: World War 2 draft registration card, 1940. Donald was 24.

In the **1940 US Census,** Donald and Dorothy lived at 205 S. Pendleton (renting). His occupation was listed as a "salesman, Stove Co." Don's death certificate in 1964 lists his occupation as "Radio and Hi-Fi Equipment." His address was 1020 W. Truman Road, Independence, Missouri. This might have been where his business was located.

> DONALD W. COOK. Donald W. Cook, 47, of 1020 West Truman Road, Independence, died yesterday at his home, apparently of a heart attack. He was a native of Independence and was a graduate of William Chrisman High School. Since 1944 he owned and operated the Don Cook Hi-Fi Stereo Music Center there. He was a member of the Reorganized Latter Day Saints Stone Church, the Independence Optimist Club, the Independence Chamber of Commerce and the Audio Engineering Society. He leaves his wife, Mrs. Dorothy Cook of the home, his parents, Mr. and Mrs. Eric Cook, 1400 West Short, Independence, and a sister, Miss Margaret Cook, New York. Services will be at 1:30 o'clock Wednesday at the Speaks Chapel; burial in Mound Grove Cemetery. Friends may call from 7 to 9 o'clock Tuesday night at the chapel.

—*The Kansas City Star,* Kansas City, Missouri, Monday, 15 Jun 1964, page 16

Donald W. Cook, Mound Grove Cemetery, Independence, Missouri, died age 47.

2. *Margaret Louise "Peggy" Cook* (1918-2003). Died at age 85. She possibly had Alzheimer's. Buried at Mound Grove Cemetery.

Peggy Cook, Mound Grove Cemetery, Independence, Missouri, died age 85.

Collage of Eric P. Cook family photos from Virginia Dungan's photo book.

Cover of booklet in which Eric Cook shares his experiences.

The following are excerpts from a booklet titled *Remember When . . .* in which residents of Resthaven (later renamed The Groves) shared experiences.

Eric Cook tells us:

"I remember one time when my father and mother had been to church and were riding in a buggy as they went home. Two of my sisters and I were in another buggy behind them. We got to a pretty good-sized hill and my father's horse tried to hold back the buggy and the hold-back strap [wrapped around the shaft of the buggy to prevent it from running up on the horse] broke, letting the buggy go down on the back of the horse. This scared him and he lunged. That pulled the buggy to the side and broke the shaft. They finally got to the bottom of the hill and the sand there stopped the buggy. My father had to do the repair job. There was binder twine to fix the shaft, and we finally got home."

Eric Cook had so many memories of fun in his childhood that he didn't know what to tell first.

"We usually made our own playthings. We used grape vines for ropes in several ways. For swings, we would get two vines rather close together. Then two of us would swing our and try to see who could jump the farthest. Then we played jump the rope with the grape vine rope. One experience we had with a natural grape vine swing—we'd go up about 15 feet above the ground as we swung out. One time my father got uneasy about this, so he got hold of it and since he was a heavy man, he jumped up and down to test it, then decided it was safe. A couple of days later my sister was swinging out over the ditch and just as she was coming back, the vine broke. When we examined the vine we found a borer or worm had gotten in it and had eaten it almost in two—so no one got hurt but that was lucky."

Eric Cook learned how to knit by watching his mother knit his socks. He tells about the process this way:

"They spun the wool yarn by making a roll of wool about the size of your little finger which was put on the spinning wheel to make yarn. I have seen her spin hundreds of yards of it. Then she would double that thread and not wind it real tight. Once I knitted a sock myself. My mother would knit the toe and heel, but I did the rest. By the way, those socks when they got too worn out to wear, she would let us take that unraveled yarn and make wool balls out of it. We had a game called the Bull Pen. There were two sides and we would take one of these balls and try to hit someone on the other side. If he got hit, he had to come to your side and the object was to getl all on your side. If you failed to hit anyone you had to get in the center which was the Bull Pen."

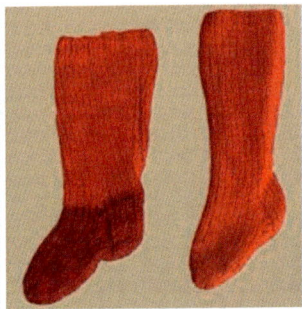

80

Eric also remembers button shoes that you had to use a button hook on. These were for good, but for work you wore brogans which were hard on your feet. Also you wore a waist which buttoned on to your pants. For everyday there were softwoven straw hats that had a shoestrings around the crown so you could adjust it to fit your head. Then for Sunday they had stiff straw hats.

Eric Cook told of digging a hole in the ground with a post hole digger, into which buckets were lowered on a rope for cooling, since he lived in Kentucky where the ice never got thick enough to store. [In northern states, the ice was cut from ponds or small lakes when the weather got cold enough to freeze it into blocks which were cut and hauled to the ice houses.]

Eric Cook remembers many things about the food in the home:

"To start with, we had what we called lightnin' bread, which is what we called white flour biscuits. Then we had corn bread. It was made by mixing corn meal with a little water and salt. Then my mother made it into a loaf—not really a loaf—but it would be formed by hand and put into a pan and baked. I especially like it when there was a hard crust. One of our staples was sorghum molasses, and it was used with the corn bread as a favorite dessert when I was young. We kept it in a barrel and it would keep all winter. Once it was so thick it had turned to sugar and we had to return it to sorghum by putting water with it.

"Hog killing time came in the winter and we put the cracklins in the corn bread and that was called 'cracklin bread.' Cracklins was hog fat which was cooked down until they were real brown, then they were ground and used in the corn bread. They were strained out of the lard before it was stored to be used for frying.

"When we butchered, the lean part of the hog was ground up and made into sausage. We could halfway preserve it by making tubes of cloth a little heavier than cheese cloth, then filled with this ground pork, then roll the whole things in a kind of flour paste on the outside which would keep the sausage for awhile, but not too long.

"The way we got the corn and wheat flour was to take the corn after it was shelled and sorted to be sure you had no bad kernels. Then you would take it to the mill, they would grind it and you would get back the corn meal you took in. Later they would just give you the amount you took in and you never knew whose corn it was. Wheat was ground in big batches and was sifted so the flour was separated from the bran—but you got back both flour and bran.

"I was thinking about the milk. We had 3 cows. I milked one of them and my older brother would milk the others. Then it was poured into a churn where the cream would rise. The clabbered milk in the bottom would be made into cottage cheese and the sour cream would be churned for butter. The dasher was a cross piece of wood on the handle and you went up and down through the cream until the butter formed."

Eric Cook begins:

"I am wondering how to start. When I was between 11 and 12, we had been living on the farm. I had gone to school there and most of the time I was the only one in class. At about this time, my father thought that my older brothers and older sister were at the place where we would need more. Because of the conditions in that school, we would need a better education. He bought a little place in a Kentucky town where situations were much better.

"I went to school there, and as a matter of fact, the school building burned down the first year I was there and we had to attend classes temporarily in a pants factory! It was Murray, Kentucky [about 25 miles north of Paris, Tennessee].

"Really, the turning point was when we moved to Independence in 1905. I was almost ready for high school. We moved here and my father, being a farmer, wanted to find a place where we could have a cow and some chickens.

"In the summer time I wanted to get something I could do to help pay my way so I went to work in a tobacco factory. I worked and the first job I had was in Murray, Kentucky. I got the big price of 33 and 1/3 cents a day.

"Of course, when we moved to Independence we got out of the tobacco area.

"In our school here, we had physical geography. It was scientific and it appealed to me, but the most interesting were the science courses. A teacher by the name of Stone was very influential in my life."

Eric Cook says:

"I remember when I first came here to Resthaven. I thought I wouldn't tell anyone my birthday, and just pay any attention to it. But, as a matter of fact, before my birthday really came, they gave me a celebration, but it was a mistake, because the date was reallty my room-mate's birthday. I remember Bro. Fred M. Smith once said, 'No one ever has by one birthday. After that they are all anniversaries.' On the 28th of February next will be my 93rd anniversary.

"The first Christmas I remember of having a tree, under it was a set of blocks—ABC blocks. I would play with them by setting them up and knock them down in rows—then pile them to see how high I could make them before they would fall.

"What might be interesting here is something that happened when I was a youngster in Tennessee. There they celebrated Christmas very much as they celebrate the 4th of July here. We had fireworks with Roman candles, skyrockets and explosions of lights. One year I got an air gun for Christmas and I thought I was on top of the world.

"On Christmas eve we'd hang our stockings and presents would be put in them. Usually I'd get an orange and nuts and Christmas candies would be in the stockings."

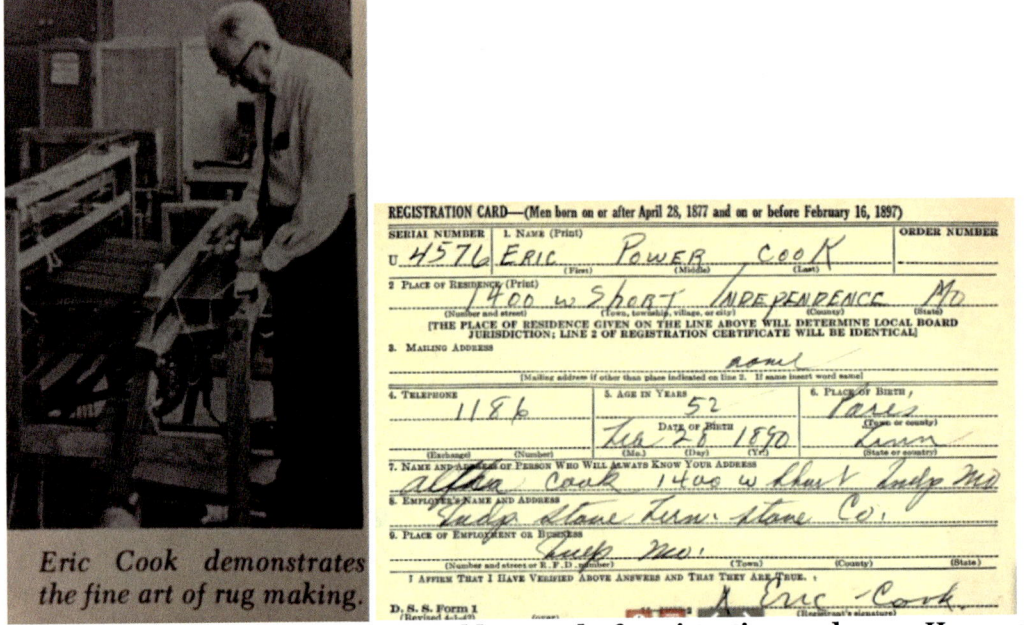

Eric Cook demonstrates the fine art of rug making.

Eric Cook at Resthaven, circa 1980s. World War 2 draft registration card, 1942. He was 52.

~~~

Gela Lela Cook Moorman

Born 31 May 1893 (Paris, Tennessee); died 27 October 1972 at age 79 (Dearborn, Missouri). Buried Knob Noster Cemetery (Knob Noster, Missouri). Married Oscar Myron Moorman 5 Jun 1918 (Independence, Missouri).

Gela was the youngest of the six Cook children. Her family belonged to the RLDS Church and attended Foundry Hill, in Puryear, Tennessee, about 10 miles north of Paris, Tennessee. She became a member of the church when she was 8 years old.

Gela Cook's baptism and confirmation certificate, Puryear, Tennessee, 8 Sep 1901.

Gela Lela Cook. Left: unknown date. Right: 1909.

Postcards to Gela Cook, 1909–1911

Front: Australian Ballot Postcard

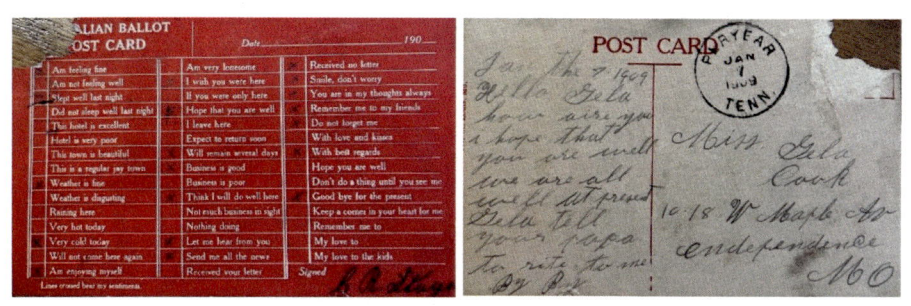

Postmark: Puryear, Tenn., Jan 7, 1909; stamp torn off

To: Miss. Gela Cook, 1018 [1028] W maple Av, Independence, MO

Jan the 7 1909

Hello Gela how are you i hope that you are well we are all well at present Gela tell your papa [Elias P. Cook] to rite to me By By [signed on front] C. R. Stagner

Editor Note: Gela would have been 15 years old at this time. She moved with her family from Henry County, Third District, Tennessee, to Missouri in 1905. The writer of this card might have been Charles Robbins Stagner (1871-1954). In the 1910 US Census, Stagner was single and living with his sister in Puryear, Tennessee.

~~~

Front: With kindest greetings and love sincere—To My Valentine

Postmark: Theodore, Ala. Feb 1910, 1 cent stamp

To: Miss. Gela Cook. Independence, 1028 W. Maple Ave., MO.

Theodore Ala Feb 21, 1910

Dear Gela, I received your card some time ago. Was glad to get it. How many Brother's and Sister's have you? My home is near the church. We have a nice Sunday School. I am Libarion of the Sunday School. I have two Brothers and two Sister. I will close. Hoping to hear from you soon. I am as ever your friend, Virdie Booker.

Editor Note: Gela was 16 at this time. The writer is likely Victoria Virdie Lee Booker, 16 years old at this time. She had two sisters and two brothers (all younger). Both women were members of the RLDS Church. Virdie's father was Willis Leonidas Booker (1845-1925). "Known as 'Uncle Tommie,' he was baptized and confirmed a member of the Reorganized Church of Jesus Christ of Latter Day Saints on 27 February 1866 at Monroe County, Alabama, by W. A. Litz. He was ordained an elder on 3 August 1867 in Monroe County by T. H. Waddel. Willis attended the Alabama branches at Lone Star and Theodore; the Missouri branches at Waconda, Knoxville, Norborne, and Far West; and the Bluff Creek, Mississippi, Branch. He was a missionary." Virdie married Garrett Easley in 1912 and she died in 1925 in Mobile, Alabama.

~~~

Front: Picture of couple by a lake in the moonlight.

Postmark: Paris, Tenn. April 15, 1910, 5 PM; 1 cent stamp

To: Miss Gela Cook, 1028 W. Maple, Ave., Independence, Mo.

Helo to Gela, how are you all this fine morning? We are dandy. All excepting Mary and she has the measeles. They broke out on her before we got to St. Louis. We made it home O.K. Grace is dandy. It stormed here last night. Tell all folks helo for me. And answer Sorry I remain as ever Pearl. I certainly wish XXX------were there. XXX------

Editor Note: This might be from Pearl Milliken, Gela's cousin. Gela's brother, Berber, married Grace Mabel Shupe (1889-1965) in 1909 in Tennessee. Mary Lane Cook (1896-1980) was also Gela's cousin.

~~~

Front: Best Wishes

Postmark: none [1911–1914?]

To: Miss Gela Cook, 1028 West Maple Ave., Independence, Mo.

Dear Gela, <u>ans soon</u>

how are you all by this time. We are all well except colds. Certainly are having some bad weather now. Our school [in Cottage, Grove, Tennessee] was out last Friday I guess you are still going to school [in Missouri]. How is Irma [Gela's sister] getting along? Yes we got your picture all Ok. It is just fine. When did you hear from Clark? I had a card not very long ago she was well then. Give my love to all. Alma

Editor Note: This card is likely from Alma (Lee Hays McVay Wallace), Gela's cousin. Clark might refer to Gela and Alma's maternal aunt, Roe Clark, who died in 1914 at age 34.

~~~

Front: Image of girl with long brown curly hair

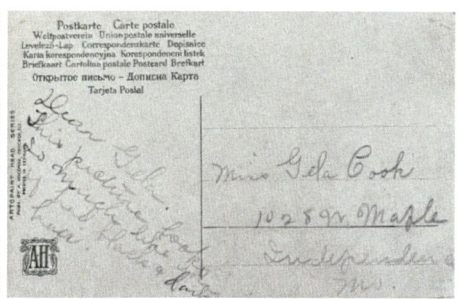

Postmark: none [about 1911]

To: Miss Gela Cook, 1028 W. Maple, Independence, Mo. Postkarte Carte postale

Dear Gela. This picture looks so much like you if had black & dark hair.

Editor Note: This postcard is similar to the card from Guy Milliken, Gela's cousin, who died in Hawaii in 1912.

~~~

Front: A Joyful Easter, boy holding basket of colored eggs

Postmark: none [about 1911]

To: Miss Gela Cook, 1028 West Maple Ave., Independence, Mo. Postkarte

Hello Gela how are you getting along in school? Study hard and learn all you can and write soon to your loving cousin. Guy Milliken

~~~

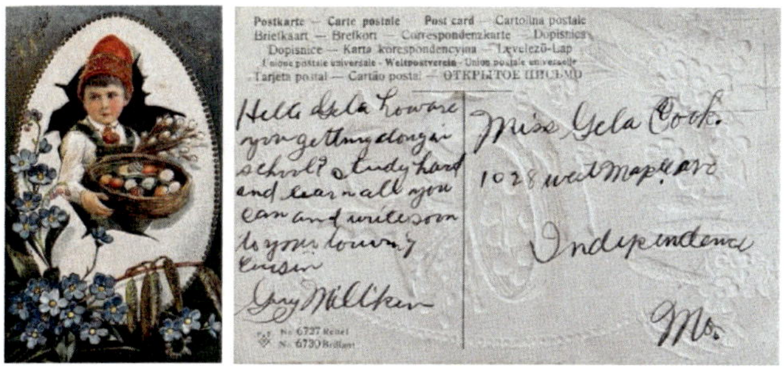

Gela Lela Cook

1910s

Gela Cook, circa 1910s.

Gela moved with her parents and siblings from Tennessee to Missouri in 1905 when she was 12. She graduated as a nurse from the Independence Sanitarium in May 1916.

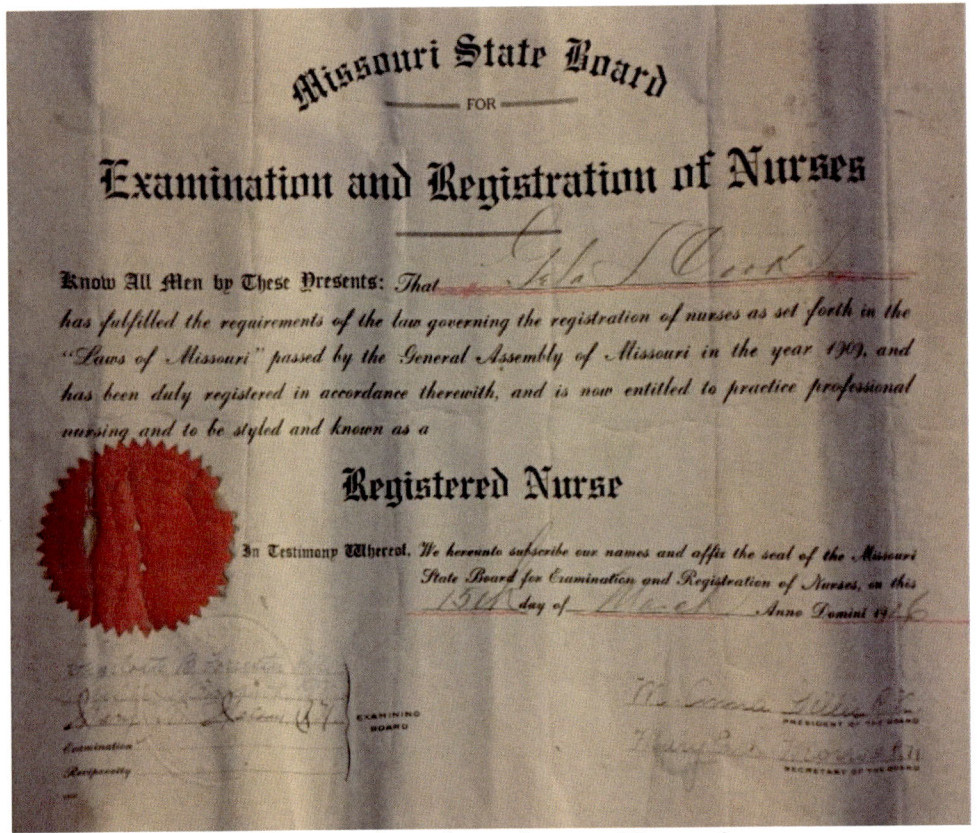

Gela L. Cook, registered nurse, Mar 1916.

Left: Gela, far left, Independence Sanitarium, 1916. Right: Gela, top row, far right.

Two years later, in June 1918, at the age of 25, she married Oscar, whom she'd met at a church reunion gathering.

Oscar and Gela Moorman, wedding day, Independence, Missouri, 5 Jun 1918.

Addresses for Oscar and Gela Cook Moorman

- 1920—1502 W. Walnut, Independence, Missouri.
- 1930-1940—1028 W. Maple, Independence, Missouri.
- Knob Noster, Missouri.

1920s

In February 1920, Gela gave birth to her first child, Virginia, in Independence, Missouri. That summer, in July, she and Virginia traveled by train to Montana, where Oscar was working to build brick silos.

Postcards from Montana, 1920

Front: 8243. Interior Broadwater Plunge Bath, Helena, Mont. **Editor Note:** Colonel Charles Broadwater built the Broadwater Hotel and Natatorium in 1889, the year Montana achieved statehood. This grand resort was the stopping place for elite travelers going to and from the national parks of Yellowstone and Glacier. The Broadwater Hot Springs Natatorium pool at 30,000 square feet, was the world's largest indoor pool. At one end of the pool giant granite boulders formed into two waterfalls, one from the Hot Springs and one from a Cold Springs. The Natatorium also sported toboggan slides, a "plunge" and observation decks. Stained-glass windows and colorful tiles covered the interior floors and walls. At night, lit from within by electric lights, the building glistened like a jewel box. An earthquake in 1935 severely damaged the Natatorium and it was soon condemned.

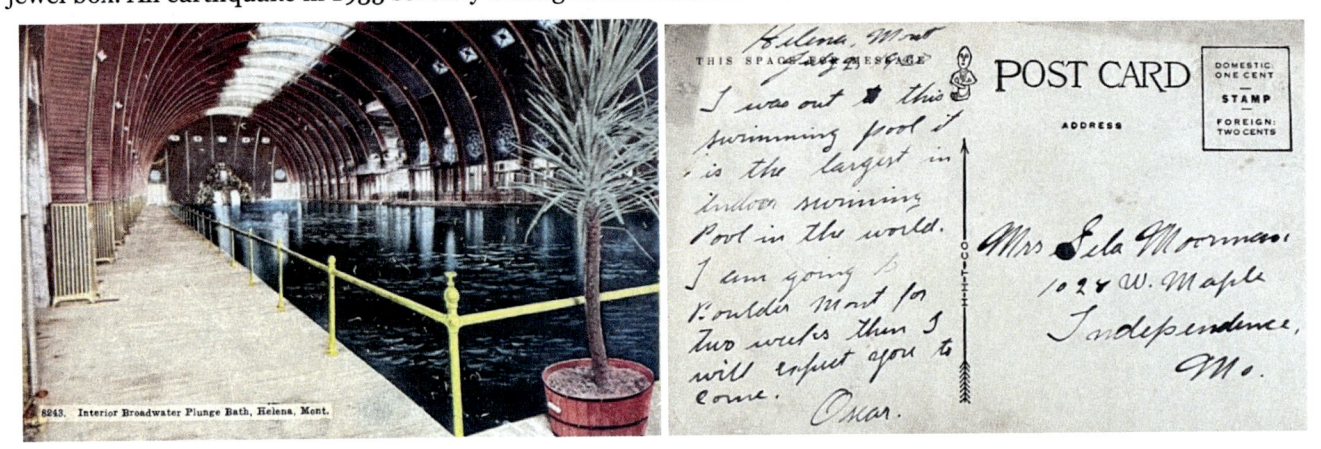

Postmark: none [2 Jul 1920]

To: Mrs. Gela Moorman, 1028 W. Maple, Independence, Mo.

Helena, Mont. July 2, 1920

I was out to this swimming pool it is the largest in indoor swimming pool in the world. I am going to Boulder Mont for two weeks then I will expect you to come. Oscar.

Editor Note: Oscar was working in Montana as a brickmason. Gela and Virginia (born in Feb 1920) joined him in July 1920, traveling by train from Kansas City, Missouri. Because there is no stamp or postmark, Oscar probably gave Gela this postcard (and the one on the next page) when she arrived

~~~

Front: Mt. Helena from Helena, Mont.

Left: Mount Helena, 2020. **Middle:** postcard view about 1920. **Right:** back of postcard.

Postmark: none [1920]

To: none [Gela Moorman]

I was up on top of this yesterday I wish you could have jumped up there for jumping is easier than climbing. It took me an hour to walk down. The view is wonnderfull. [Oscar]

Editor Note: At 5,461 feet, Mount Helena looms over the state capital of Montana. The 1906 trail is the most direct route, passing a ponderosa forest, limestone cliffs, and the Devil's Kitchen cave.

~~~

Front: I hope you'll have bushels of fun—CHRISTMAS.

Postmark: Helena, Mont., Dec 1920, 3 PM; 1 cent stamp

To: Miss Virginia Moorman, 1028 W. Maple Avenue, Independence, Mo.

Merry Christmas, Ginger.

Mary Marie, 310 Ninth Ave, Helena, Mont.

Editor Note: This would have been Virginia's first Christmas. She and her parents were in Montana in July 1920. This was sent to the home address in Independence, Missouri. Note that the card calls her "Ginger," but she wasn't traditionally known by that name. It's unknown who Mary Marie was.

~~~

1921

In March 1921, Gela gave birth to Enid Eloise Moorman in Independence, Missouri.

Postcards to Gela Moorman, 1923–1927

Front: 11109-16 Bird's-eye view, looking north, showing Clifton Hotel, Steel Arch Bridge and American falls of Niagara. **Editor Note:** The original Clifton Hotel, built in 1831, was destroyed by fire in 1898. It was rebuilt and had five stories. The second hotel was destroyed by fire in 1932 and never rebuilt. He Steel Arch Bridge connected Canada to the United States. It collapsed in 1938 after a massive amount of ice came over the falls and pushed against the bridge. The replacement Rainbow Bridge was opened in 1941.

Postmark: Niagara Falls, Ont., Sep 14, 1923, 6:30 AM; 2 cent stamp Canada

To: Mrs. G. Moorman, 1312 W Kensington, Independence, Mo

Made in England

Friday

We Stopped over a day to see the falls here. Leave to nite for N. Y. Laddi [Oscar]

Editor Note: This address on Kensington is where Gela's sister, Irma Cook Stover, lived.

~~~

Front: Best Christmas Wishes

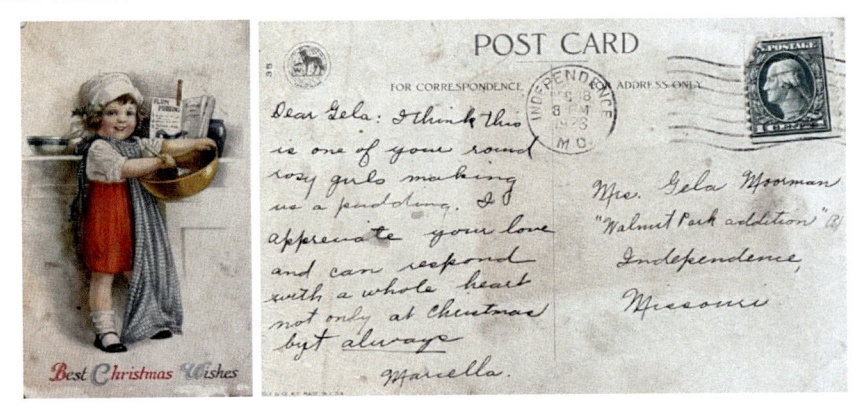

Postmark: Independence, MO, Dec 18, 1923, 8 PM; 1 cent stamp

To: Mrs. Gela Moorman, "Walnut Park addition" (?), Independence, Missouri

Dear Gela: I think this is one of your round rosy girls [referring to Virginia and Enid?] making us a pudding. I appreciate your love and can respond with a whole heart not only at Christmas but <u>always</u> Marcella.

Editor Note: This writer is likely Marcella Nevada Schenck (1887-1953) who was six years older than Gela. She was an author of several books (*Mr. Saucy at the Zoo* and *Jimmy Umphrey*) and an artist. She was a primary teacher in the Lamoni, Iowa, schools in the 1930s. Marcella and Gela both belonged to the RLDS Church. The "Walnut Park addition" is probably where Gela lived at 831 S. Leslie Street.

~~~

Front: 315:—Horseshoe Falls from *Maid of the Mist,* Niagara Falls. **Editor Note:** The Maid of the Mist has operated as a tour boat at the base of Niagara Falls since 1846. It used to operate from the Canadian side, but lost the contract in 2009. In 1997, Maid of the Mist VII was in operation. It carries up to 600 passengers. In 2020, two fully electric boats were launched.

Postmark: Buffalo, NY, Sta B, Jun 19, 1925, 12 M; 2 cent stamp

To: Mrs. Gela C. Moorman, 289 Brighton Beach Ave., Coney Island, N.Y.

6/19/25

Dear Gela, Please know I thoroughly appreciated your two long letters & I'm going to write you when I get back from Pearls [maybe in Tennessee?]. You never received one long letter I wrote to your old address [in Missouri or New Jersey]. Go to Youngstown [Ohio—about 185 miles from Buffalo] Monday for a week or ten days. We made a change of address also. Moved May 1st to 402 Baynes Street [Buffalo, New York] so have been busy settling down in new quarters. Hope all are well. Will write at length later. Lovingly K.N.W. Buffalo, N.Y.

Editor Note: Pearl might be Gela's cousin, Pearl Milliken, living in Paris, Tennessee, in 1910. Unknown who KNW is. It's not known why Gela was in New York at this time—perhaps because of Oscar's work. Virginia would have been 5 years old and Enid would have been 4 years old.

~~~

Front: A Merry Christmas

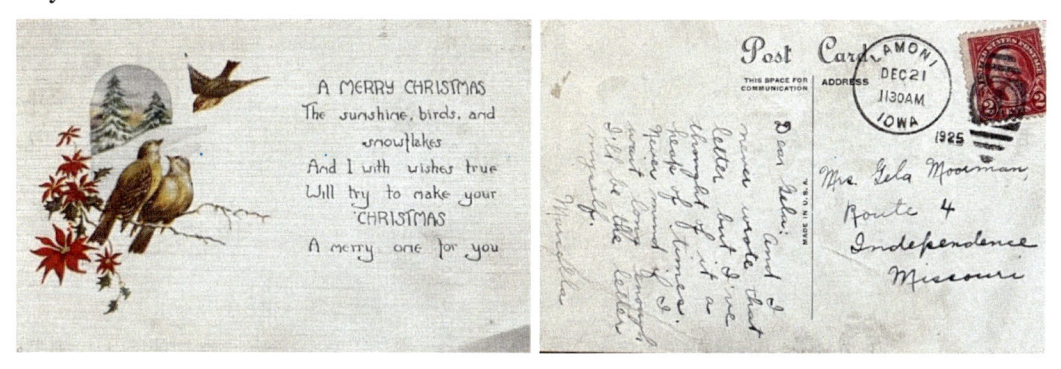

Postmark: Lamoni, Iowa, Dec 21, 1925, 11:30 AM; 2 cent stamp

To: Mrs. Gela Moorman, Route 4, Independence, Missouri

Dear Gela: And I never wrote that letter but I've thought of it a heap of times. Never mind if I wait long enough I'll be the letter myself. Marcella [Schenck]

~~~

Front: Steamer "Alexander Hamilton" of the Hudson River Day Line. **Editor Note:** *Alexander Hamilton* was one of the last sidewheel steamboats to be built for the Hudson River Day Line in 1924. Her last voyage was 6 Sep 1971. It was added to the National Register of Historic Places on March 25, 1977. On 8 Nov 1977, a storm blew up and the Hamilton sank at her pier. Although several groups tried valiantly to raise the funds, the Hamilton never floated again. The remains of the vessel are located adjacent to the Naval Weapons Station Earle pier in Middletown Township, New Jersey.

Bear Mountain rises from the west bank of the Hudson River in New York state.

Postmark: none [1926?]

To: Mrs. Gela Moorman, 831 S. Lesslie [Leslie] St, Independence, Moo

Monday

Harry, Eugene & I [Harry Moorman was Oscar's brother. Eugene Moorman was Oscar's paternal uncle.] are on our way up to Bear Mt. its raining so we wont have such a good time as last year. Laddi [Oscar] RFD #4 Box 91.

~~~

Front: Japanese Tea House, Estate of Mrs. O. H. P. Belmont, Newport, R.I. **Editor Note:** Alva Vanderbilt divorced William Vanderbilt in 1895. She then married Oliver Hazard Perry Belmont, a US representative from New York. After he died in 1908, she built a Chinese Tea House, modeled after a 12th-century Song Dynasty temple, on the seaside cliffs and hosted rallies for women's right to vote.

Left: After extensive renovations, circa 2020.

Postmark: Newport, R.I., Aug 4, 1926, 9 PM

To: Mrs. Gila Moorman, ~~831 So. Leslie St.,~~ 1028 Maple, Independence, Mo.

24 Walnut St., Newport, R.I.

Dear Gila, I spent just a week in N.Y. when I finally reached there. Took one case, then brot Alice up here for the Summer to help her regain her health which was much run down. We are only 2 blocks from the shore so we spend most of our time in the water. Alice is fine now. My son's boat is also anchored here for a short stay so we have some pleasant visits too. Hope you all are as healthy & happy as we are. My love to the little girlies. Anson C. Foy

Editor Note: Unknown people mentioned in this postcard. The family had evidently moved from Leslie Street to Maple Avenue.

~~~

Postcards from Altha Cook, 1926

Front: Indianola Presbyterian Church, Columbus, Ohio. **Editor Note:** The cornerstone for this church, designed by architect Charles Inscho, was laid 28 Mar 1915. Located at 1970 Waldeck Avenue, two blocks from The Ohio State University, it continues to function as an active church in 2022.

Postmark: Columbus, Ohio, Aug 19, 1926, 2:30 PM; no stamp

To: Miss Virginia Moorman, 205 S. Pendleton, Indep., Mo

Aug. 19, 1926

Dear Virginia; How are you? Playing and having a good time I hope. We are enjoying ourselves. Tell Mother [Gela Moorman] to give <u>worm</u> medicine to Donald & Margaret [Peggy]. Lovingly, Aunt Altha

Editor Note: Altha, married to Eric Cook, was Gela's sister-in-law. She was also Virginia's aunt. Altha and Eric had two children. Don would have been 10 at this time and Peggy would have been 8. This card indicates that Gela was living at Altha and Eric's house to care for Don and Peggy. Gela's girls were probably staying here also. Virginia would have been 6 and Enid would have been 5.

There is a series of postcards that Altha sent to her home address on Pendleton while on vacation in 1926. The itinerary took them to Columbus, Ohio; Philadelphia, Pennsylvania; New York City, Niagara Falls; Ontario (Canada); Detroit, Michigan; and St. Louis, Missouri.

~~~

Front: Sesqui-Centennial International Exposition, Philadelphia, PA. 147. Administration Building, League Island Navy Yard. **Editor Note:** The Sesqui-Centennial International Exposition of 1926 was a world's fair in Philadelphia, Pennsylvania. Its purpose was to celebrate the 150th anniversary of the signing of the US Declaration of Independence, and the 50th anniversary of the 1876 Centennial Exposition. It opened on 31 May 1926 and ran through 30 Nov 1926. *Variety* dubbed it "America's Greatest Flop" with a loss of $20 million by August 1926. The exposition ended up unable to cover its debts and was placed into receivership in 1927.

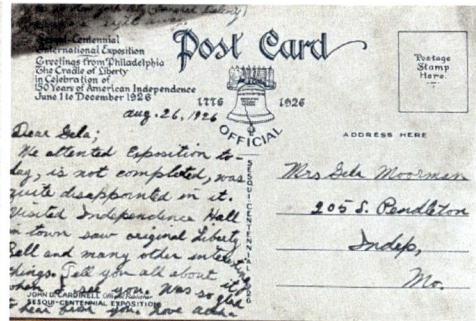

Postmark: none [26 Aug 1926]

To: Mrs. Gela Moorman, 205 S. Pendleton, Indep, Mo.

Aug. 26, 1926

Dear Gela; We attented Exposition today, is not completed, was quite disappointed in it. Visited Independence Hall in town [Philadelphia] saw original Liberty Bell and many other interesting things. Tell you all about it when I see you. Was so glad to hear from you. Love Altha Write to New York at (General Delivery) with more right away.

~~~

Front: Times Building, New York City. **Editor Note:** One Times Square, also known as Times Building, is a 25-story, 363-foot-high skyscraper designed by Cyrus L. W. Eidlitz. Built in 1903-1904 as the headquarters of the *New York Times,* the paper's owner renamed the area "Times Square." In 1913, the *Times* moved its headquarters but retained ownership of the tower. Due to the large amount of revenue generated by its signage, One Times Square is considered one of the most valuable advertising locations in the world.

Postmark: none [27 Aug 1926]

To: Mrs. Oscar Moorman, 205 S. Pendleton, Independence, Mo.

Aug. 27, 1926 Dear Gela; Does this look natural? It is beginning to look that way to me, and we only got here yesterday. We want to go to Coney Island [amusement district] soon also see Statue of Liberty [on Liberty Island in New York Harbor] and Metropolitan Museum [of Art, also called "the Met"], and Bronx Park [home of the Bronx Zoo and the Botanical Garden] beside central park, also take ride on Subway. Well I was so happy to get your letter. Is Oscar there yet? Love to you and babies. [Altha] Address us Detroit, Michigan (general delivery)

~~~

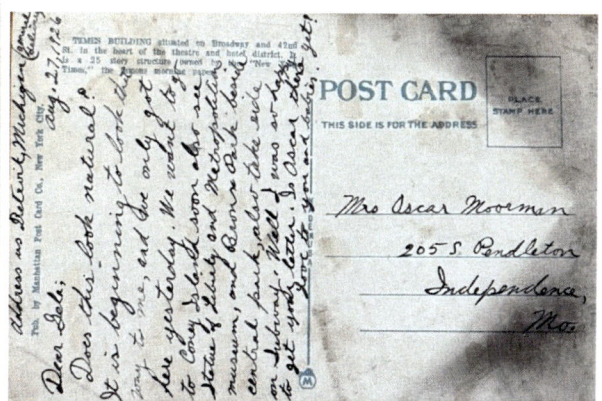

Front: The New Boardwalk, Coney Island, N.Y. **Editor Note:** The Riegelmann Boardwalk, named for Brooklyn borough president Edward J. Riegelmann, also known as Coney Island Boardwalk, is a 2.7-mile long boardwalk on the southern shore of Coney Island, facing the Atlantic Ocean. It was designed by Philip Farley, opened in 1923, and had extensions added in 1926 and 1941. It is operated by New York City. It's raised 13-14 feet above sea level and is about 80 feet wide for most of its length.

Postmark: none [30 Aug 1926]

To: Mrs. Oscar Moorman, 205 S. Pendleton, Indep, Mo

Aug. 30 [1926]

Dear Gela; We leave for Niargia Falls [New York] today but address mail to Detroit Mich (general delivery) We had quite a day yesterday but the boat ride [to the Statue of Liberty?] was the best. We sure live on a busy st. Indep. will surely be quiet. My I will be glad to see all. Love Altha Tell your babies I send love.

~~~

Front: Bear Mountain Bridge Road, N.Y. Showing bridge in the distance. **Editor Note:** The Peekskill Bear Mountain Bridge Road is the Eastern approach to the bridge. Is a newly constructed road, blasted out of the lofty sides of Anthony's Nose and Manito Mountains, and commanding the most picturesque views of the Hudson River. Its greatest elevation is more than 400 feet above the river. This road connects the Bridge with the Albany Post Road, and is over three miles long.

Postmark: none [1 Sep 1926], 2 cent stamp

To: Mrs. Gela Moorman, 205 S. Pendleton, Independence, Mo.

Albany, Sept. 1

Dear Gela; The beauty is beyond words we leave for Niargia Fall [New York] in a few minutes. Write to St. Louis [Missouri] next. Love to all. And tt Altha.

~~~

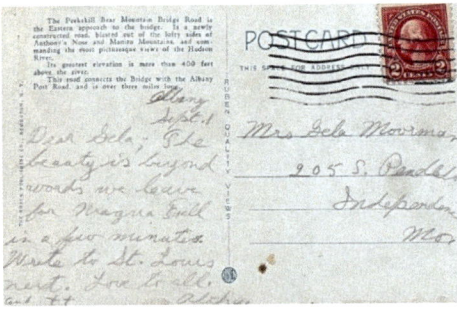

Front: A: American Falls from Below by Illumination. Niagara Falls. © Tates 23861

NIAGARA FALLS BY ILLUMINATION Visitors now find Niagara more beautiful than ever. New radiance has been cast over it. It is a radiance that can be turned on or off at the switch of a button. As turned on each night it consists of a battery of a billion candle power which are so concealed in the foliage that they in no way mar the scenery, yet they work for hours each night flooding and lighting both the vision of the Falls and the mists above. Think what has been done to accomplish this. Power was taken from the Falls themselves and turned back upon these Falls in the form of light so that Niagara is forced to beautify itself.

Editor Note: Beginning in 1860, the falls were illuminated with 200 Bengal lights (a kind of firework that gives off a blue flame) for special events. In the 1920s, 24 new arc lights were installed permanently, which led to the creation of the Niagara Falls Illumination Board in 1925 to ensure the management, operation, and maintenance of the illumination lights.

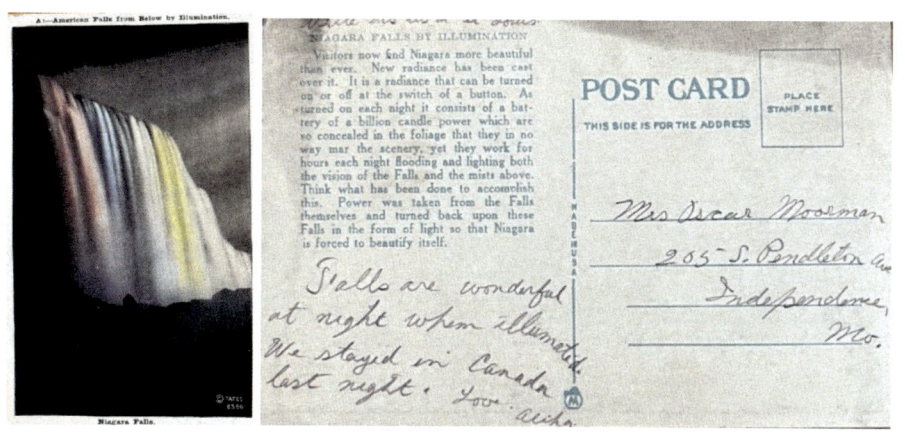

Postmark: none [Sep 1926]

To: Mrs. Oscar Moorman, 205 S. Pendleton Ave, Independence, Mo.

Falls are wonderful at night when illuminated. We stayed in Canada last night. Love, Altha Write to us at St. Louis [Missouri].

~~~

Front: Westminster Hospital, London, Ont. **Editor Note:** Construction of Westminster Psychopathic Hospital began in 1918 and was opened for patients in May 1920. As a military hospital, it was used primarily to treat and rehabilitate veterans with psychological injuries and shell shock suffered during World War I. Soon the need for medical and surgical treatment for veterans was recognized and, by a policy change in 1929, such wards were established and it was renamed Westminster Hospital. The hospital expanded during World War II to treat the injured and sick from nearby training camps. Following World War II, the focus returned to long-term and acute care for veterans with disabilities. Westminster Hospital merged with Victoria Hospital in 1977 and became known as Victoria Hospital—Westminster Campus. In 1980, Parkwood Hospital assumed responsibility for the care of veterans.

Postmark: London, Canada, Sep 4, 1926, 12:30 PM; 2 cent Canada

To: Mrs. Oscar Moorman, 205 S. Pendleton, Indep, Mo.

London, Canada, Sept. 4, 1926

Dear Gela; We stayed alnight here. Expect to stay in Detroit [Michigan] alnight and mabe part of tomorrow. Hope we hear from you. Love, Altha

~~~

1926–1929

In the late 1920s, about 1927, Oscar, Gela, Virginia, and Enid moved to New Jersey, probably to be near where Oscar was working. Gela gave birth to Eleanor in Apr 1928 in New Jersey.

Left: Enid, Gela, and Virginia, probably Missouri, circa 1926. Right: Gela and Virginia, Boston, 1928.

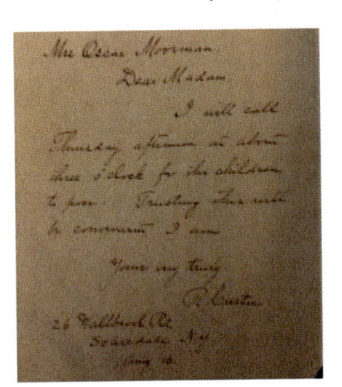

Mrs. Oscar Moorman
Dear Madam
I will call Thursday afternoon at about three o'clock for the children to pose. Trusting this will be convenient. I am
Yours very truly
R. Curtis
26 Wallbrook [Walbrooke] Rd
Scarsdale N.Y.
Aug 10. [c. 1927]

Editor Note: Robert W. Curtis, at this address, appears in the *Annual Register of the College of the City of New York*. He is listed as an officer of instruction in the Chemistry Building in 1918 and 1919.

Postcards, 1928–1929

Front: Lucas County Court House and McKinley Monument, Toledo, Ohio. **Editor Note:** The Lucas County Courthouse is an architecturally significant courthouse in downtown Toledo, Ohio, located at 700 Adams Street. The courthouse first opened in 1897. It was designed by David L. Stine. The courthouse was added to the National Register of Historic Places in 1973. William McKinley Jr. was born in Ohio in 1843. He was the 25th US president. He was assassinated in 1901. The sculptor was Hermon A. MacNeil of New York. It was unveiled in 1906.

Left: 2018 image of courthouse and monument.

Postmark: Findlay, Ohio, Jun 11, 1928, 7:30 AM; 2 cent stamp

To: Mrs. O. Moorman, 764 Undercliff Ave, Edgewater, New Jersey

Dear Gela: I arrived in Toledo O.K. I'm waiting for the Findlay train now. Sorry I didn't see Oscar yesterday goodbye, but we couldn't find him. Tell Enid to hurry up and get over the measels. With Love, Flo.

Editor Note: Toledo, Ohio, is south of Detroit, Michigan, on the western shore of Lake Erie. Findlay, Ohio, is about 45 miles south of Toledo, Ohio. Flo might be Florence Geneva Moorman, Oscar's youngest sister and Gela's sister-in-law. She was single at this time and married Jack Guy in 1933. She might have missed Oscar in New Jersey to tell him goodbye. Enid was 7 years old at this time. There is no mention about Virginia or Eleanor and if they also got the measels.

~~~

Front: It may sound big, but here it is. AT LOW BANKS. **Editor Note:** Lowbanks, Ontario, Canada, is an unincorporated community about 30 miles west of Buffalo, New York. It's located on the northern shore of Lake Erie. The writer of this postcard lives in Welland, Ontario, about 25 miles from Lowbanks. Welland is about 400 miles from Edgewater, New Jersey.

Postmark: Ont., Au [1927], 2 cent Canada

To: Mrs. O. Mormon [sic], 756 Undercliff Ave. Edgewater, N.J.

Dear Mrs. Moorman, I am enjoying it here had a letter from Mr. [Robert W.] Curtis saying to leave my address with you so he can send me the picture. It is 212 Maple Ave Welland Ont c/o Char Bricker. Love Joel

Editor Note: See previous R. Curtis note to Gela Moorman to arrange for photographs for her children. This postcard from Joel sounds like he was in some of the pictures and would like a copy. It's likely that he was vacationing in New Jersey. There is a Charles Bricker who lived in Welland. In the 1921 Census of Canada, he's listed as a bricklayer and a member of the "Latter-day Saint" church. Perhaps Joel was friends with one of the Bricker children or was working with Charles.

~~~

Front: Campbell's at Gratiot, Ohio, Route 40, Rooms for Tourists. **Editor Note:** Gratiot, Ohio, is a village in the middle of Ohio. In the 2010 census, there were 221 people living here. Nothing can be found online about this store in Gratiot.

Postmark: none [1929]; 2 cent stamp

To: Fritz Kholer, 764 Undercliff A., Edgewater, N.J.

Dear Fritz, We are home safly this house (on the front) is where we staded one night. ~~Your~~ Virginia M. Moorman

Editor Note: The Moorman family was probably driving from New Jersey to Missouri. Gratiot is about 500 miles from Edgewater, New Jersey. It would have been about 700 more miles home to Independence, Missouri.

The address to Fritz Kholer is the same as where the Moorman family stayed. It's unclear if Fritz lived there as a tourist or as a permanent resident. Virginia would have been 9 at the time this was written. On the next page is a postcard from Enid to Fritz, written by Virginia. Enid would have been 8 at this time.

There is a Fritz Irwin Koeller from Wisconsin, who was born in 1920. He would have been near Virginia and Enid's age.

~~~

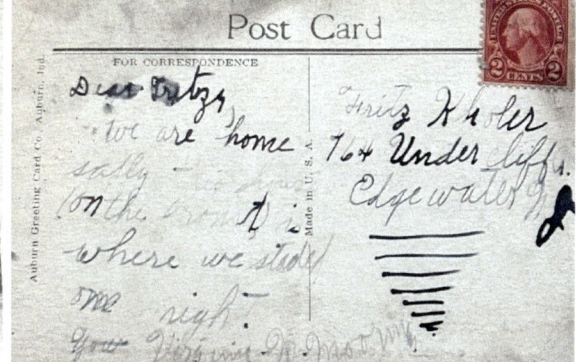

Front: 37: Colonel Swope Monument, Swope Park, Kansas City. **Editor Note:** The Thomas Hunton Swope Memorial was dedicated in 1918 and Swope's body is buried there under an inscribed stone. The site overlooks the lagoon and the entire park. The lions and decorative bronze were done by Charles Keck. The U-shaped colonnade consisted of 12 columns, 14 feet tall. Eight bronze medallions depict a species of tree found in the park. A 6-foot fountain was added in 1922 in front of the monument. See photo below.

Postmark: none [11 Nov 1929]; 2 cent stamp

To: Fritz Kholer, 764 Under Cliff, Edgewater, New Jersey

My Friend Fritz, This is Armistice day [later known as Veterans Day]. We get school of to day. We had a nice juroney home. Enid M. Written by Virginia

Editor Note: This postcard was probably written in November as it references Armistice Day. It's not clear when the family might have traveled from New Jersey home to Missouri. Virginia would have been 9, Enid was 7, and Eleanor was 1.

See previous page for information about Fritz.

~~~

Postcards, 1930–1937

Front: Making Pottery, Pueblo of San Ildefonso, New Mexico. **Editor Note:** The Pueblo de San Ildefonso history dates to AD 1300 when the people from Bandelier moved to the current location next to the Rio Grande. Before this, they had come from Mesa Verde in southern Colorado. Today the Pueblo consists of over 60,000 acres and has an enrollment of approximately 750 people, located north of Santa Fe along the Rio Grande Valley. The Pueblo is known for its traditional black on black pottery, a highly polished finish and black matte design, red and polychrome pottery and painters, jewelry makers, weavers, carvers, seamstresses, and moccasin makers. The Spaniards named the Tribes/Pueblos after patron saints. San Ildefonso was named after Saint Ildefonsus, an archbishop of Toledo, Spain.

Postmark: Albuquerque, NM, May 16, 1930, no stamp

To: Mrs. Oscar Moorman, 1028 W. Maple Ave., Independence, Mo.

Dear Girlie, We just got off here and saw a bunch of Pueblo Indians. Quite interesting. Making good time were in mts. All night. It is clear here. Rained most al day yesterday. Bless your heart the dress was beautiful but you should not have worked so late. How are you do hope better I love you dearly. Will write later. We will be in Los Angeles this time tomorrow. Lovingly, Altha

Editor Note: Altha, married to Eric Cook, was Gela's sister-in-law. There is a series of postcards from Altha during this May 1930 trip to the West Coast. They visited New Mexico; Long Beach and San Diego, California.

~~~

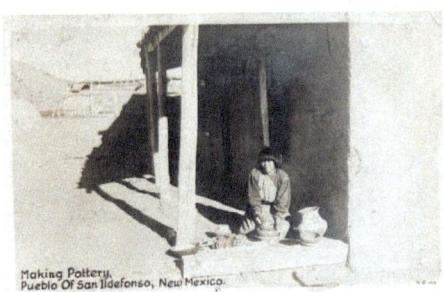

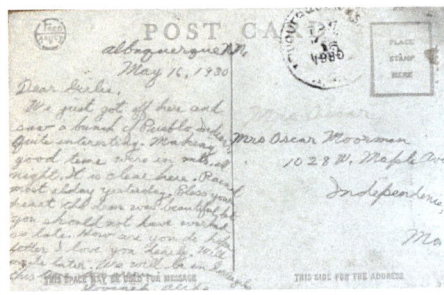

Front: High Tide, Long Beach, CA. **Editor Note:** Long Beach is a coastal city and port in southern California. It was incorporated in 1897. It's about 20 miles south of Los Angeles.

Postmark: Long Beach, Calif, May [18] 1930, 10 AM, 1 cent stamp, partially torn off

To: Mrs. Oscar Moorman, 1028 W. Maple, Indep., Mo.

Long beach Calif. May 18, 1930

Dear Gela; How would you like to ride these breakers? I love to watch people do it. This is a beautiful place, lovely weather but cool out in morning and night. We have heat in apt. then. Live on Ocean Blvd. Lovingly, Altha, Lovely and warm during day but a little cool in evenings.

Editor Note: Ocean Blvd. starts in downtown Long Beach and stretches along the waterfront (Pacific Ocean) to the Peninsula and Alamitos Park.

~~~

Front: 4627 La Jolla Beach and Yacht Club, La Jolla, San Diego, California. **Editor Note:** Opened in 1927 as the La Jolla Beach and Yacht Club, it was purchased by F. W. Kellogg in 1935 and expanded to include tennis courts, a swimming pool, and apartments and renamed the La Jolla Beach and Tennis Club. In 2022, the resort includes a restaurant and hotel and continues to be operated by the Kellogg family.

Postmark: San Diego, Calif. Jul 8, 1930, 8:30 PM; 1 cent stamp

To: Mrs. Oscar Moorman, 1028 W. Maple Ave. Independence, Mo.

La Jolla, Calif. July 7, 1930

Dear Gela; Here we are at the Yatch Club getting ready to eat under one of the umbrellas you see near building. We have been reading on beach. It is a little cool to go in today although many are in. Are you having a nice time this summer. Heard you were in Smithville [Missouri]. I am feeling some better now. Love, Altha

~~~

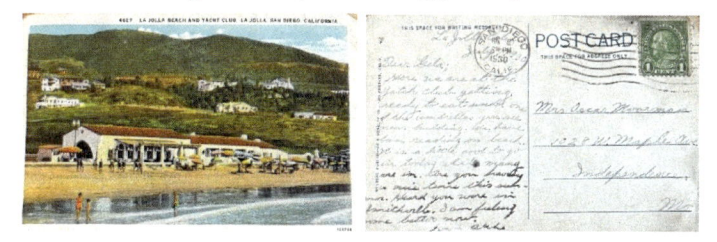

Front: 4569 Union Depot, Atchison, Topeka & Santa Fe Ry., San Diego and Arizona Ry., San Diego, Calif. **Editor Note:** Santa Fe Depot is a union station built by the Atchison, Topeka and Santa Fe Railway and opened in 1915. The station is listed on the National Register of Historic Places and is a San Diego Historic Landmark. Its architecture, particularly the signature twin domes, is often echoed in the design of modern buildings in downtown San Diego. The historic depot is still an active transportation center.

Postmark: Los Angeles, TR73, Jul 28, 1930, Air Mail, 5 cents in stamps

To: Mrs. Oscar Moorman, 1028 W. Maple, Independence, Mo.

San Diego, Cal., July 28.

My Dear Gela; Mabe this will reach you before I do. No dear I never heard about the baby having pneumonia. Heard once, she was rather cross but didn't know the cause. Please forgive me I am so sorry and surely glad she is O.K now. Leave in 5 min. Love, Altha

Editor Note: The "baby" mentioned in this postcard might have been Gela's youngest daughter, Eleanor, who would have been 2 at this time.

~~~

Front: Capital City Club, Atlanta, GA. **Editor Note:** This private club was chartered in 1883 as a social organization. The downtown Atlanta club is located at 114 Peachtree Street. Its Georgian Revival style was originally four stories and a fifth story was added later (see photo on right).

Left: Capital City Club, 2009.

Postmark: Atlanta, GA, Sta. B. Jun 22, 1931, 2:30 PM; 1 cent stamp

To: Mrs. Oscar Moorman, 1028 West Maple Ave, Independence, Missouri.

6/21/31

Having a nice time. Wish you were with us. Love, Pearl. It is surely hot here.

Editor Note: Pearl might be Ina Pearl Milliken Wallace, Gela's cousin. Pearl and her husband, Victor, lived in Symsonia, Kentucky, about 380 miles from Atlanta, Georgia.

~~~

Front: Above Timberline on Pikes Peak, Colorado. **Editor Note:** Pikes Peak is the highest summit of the southern front range of the Rocky Mountains in North America. The ultra-prominent 14,115-foot fourteener is located in Pike National Forest, 12 miles west of Colorado Springs, Colorado.

Postmark: Colorado Springs, Colo. Aug 16, 1931, 9 AM; 1 cent stamp

To: Mrs. Oscar Moorman, 1028 W. Maple Ave, Independence, Mo.

Colorado Springs, Aug. 16, 1931

My Dear Gela; I surely planned to see you before I left but it was very late when I finished packing. We are having a nice time leaving for Santa Fe, N.M. this morning it is now 4-30 A.M. Lovingly, Altha Hope you are getting steadily well.

Editor Note: Usually Altha writes several postcards when she is away, but this is the only one from 1931. It's unknown why Gela had been sick.

~~~

Front: Prometheus Fountain in Rockefeller Center, New York City

FOUNTAIN IN ROCKEFELLER CENTER, NEW YORK CITY: The Prometheus Fountain in the Sunken Plaza in ROCKEFELLER CENTER. Designed by Paul Manship, distinguished American sculptor, the bronze fountain group depicts Prometheus, legendary contributor of fire, bearing the gift down to mankind. Prometheus, the central figures is two and one-half times life size. Smaller figures in the rear are symbolized to represent the people of th earth. The two basins of the Fountain are of polished Deer Island granite and the back wall is of read Balmoral granite. **Editor Note:** Prometheus, the 18-foot-tall, eight-ton, gilded cast bronze sculpture, was created in 1934.

Left: Prometheus, 2014.

Postmark: Brooklyn, N.Y., Dec 18, 1936, 10 A.M., 1 cent stamp

To: Mrs. Gela Moorman, 1028 W Maple, Independence, Mo.

Thursday I am staying all week [in New York]. And will leave here Sunday Morning 10. a.m. Ankle better. Its raining to night hope we can work rest of week. Will write latter. O.M. [Oscar Moorman] I forgot to mail this Wed.

Editor Note: Oscar frequently worked out of town as a brick mason.

~~~

Front: Surf after a Storm. Greetings from Christmas Cove, Maine. **Editor Note:** Christmas Cove is a village on the south end of Rutherford Island in Maine. Legend says that Captain John Smith explored the coast and named this area Christmas Cove when he visited it on Christmas Day.

Postmark: Christmas Cove, Maine. July 18, 1937, 6 AM; 1 cent stamp

To: Mr and Mrs Oscar Moorman, 1028 W. Maple, Indep., Missouri

Hello all: Say, you should be here, this is really some grand country. H. has been days sea fishing and caught plenty. As Ever Harry & Kay [Moorman]

Editor Note: Harry Moorman was Oscar's brother and Gela's brother-in-law. He and his wife Kay lived in Brooklyn, New York, about 400 miles from Christmas Cove.

~~~

Front: 550 Balanced and Steamboat Rocks, Garden of the Gods, Pikes Peak Region, Colorado. BALANCED ROCK AND STEAMBOAT ROCK. The Steamboat Rock in connection with the Balanced Rock is one of the famous features of the Garden of the Gods that has been visited for tens of years. Hundreds of thousands of people have climbed upon its "Deck" to survey the region roundabout. The road entering the Garden of the Gods from the west passes directly between the two rocks. **Editor Note:** The rock was once privately owned, and tourists climbed on the rock, but climbing is now prohibited. Balanced Rock is a 35-foot, 700-ton, sandstone red rock made up of hematite, coarse sand, silica, and gravel.

Left: 1950s, when tourists could still climb on the rock. Right: 2010 image.

Postmark: Colorado Springs, Colo., Jul 19, 1937, 9:30 AM; 1 cent stamp

To: Mrs. Oscar Moorman, 1028 West Maple, Independence, Missouri.

Sun. July 18th 1937 On top of Pikes Peak now & feeling good. Love, Pearl.

Editor Note: Pearl is likely Ina Pearl Milliken Wallace, Gela's cousin.

~~~

Front: Greetings from Fulton, KY. **Editor Note:** Fulton, originally known as Pontotoc, was established in 1847 and renamed Fulton in 1861. It was once known as the "Banana Capital of the World," because 70 percent of imported bananas to the US used to be shipped from South America to New Orleans and then through the city. Fulton had the only ice house on the route north to Chicago. Bananas were laid on top of ice in the rail cars to be shipped north.

Postmark: Paducah, KY, Aug 4, 1937, 10 AM; 1 cent stamp

To: Mrs. Oscar Moorman, 1028 W Maple Ave, Independence, Mo

Aug 4, 1937

Well I am at Pearls just got up & Victor is gone but will be back soon so I will drop you a card and wait till I get home to tell all the news. I left Ethel [in Cottage Grove, Tennessee] better than Monday Alma busy as a bee & Minnie says she is better Pearls are well & looking fine we are going to Fulton today. Love Irma. [Cook Stover]

Editor Note: This postcard is from Irma Cook Stover to her younger sister, Gela Cook Moorman. Irma was staying with Ina Pearl Milliken Wallace, Irma and Gela's cousin. Pearl was married to Victor Wallace and they lived in Symsonia, Kentucky, about 15 miles south of Paducah, Kentucky. The trip to Fulton, Kentucky, would be about 40 miles south of Symsonia. Many of the Cook relatives were from the Fulton area and also from Paris, Tennessee, which was about 40 miles south of Fulton. Ethel (Nancy Shell Cloys), Minnie (May Hays Olive), and Alma (Lee Hays McVay Wallace) were cousins of Irma and Gela—they all probably lived in Cottage Grove, Tennessee, about 60 miles south of Symsonia. Their mother (Eugenia "Jennie" Porter Milliken Shell Hays, who died in 1920) was a sister to Irma and Gela's mother (Sarah Elizabeth "Ballie/Sallie Beth" Milliken, who died in 1921).

~~~

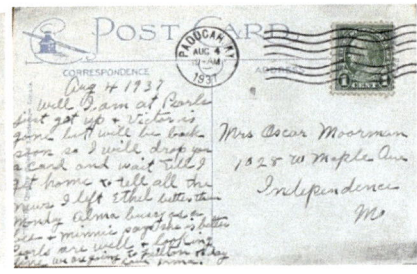

Front: Kentucky Lake near Benton, Ky. **Editor Note:** Kentucky Lake is a major navigable reservoir along the Tennessee River in Kentucky and Tennessee. It was created in 1944 by the Tennessee Valley Authority's impounding of the Tennessee River via Kentucky Dam for flood control and hydroelectric power. The small town of Benton, known as Kentucky Lake's Downtown, lies in the far western part of the Bluegrass state.

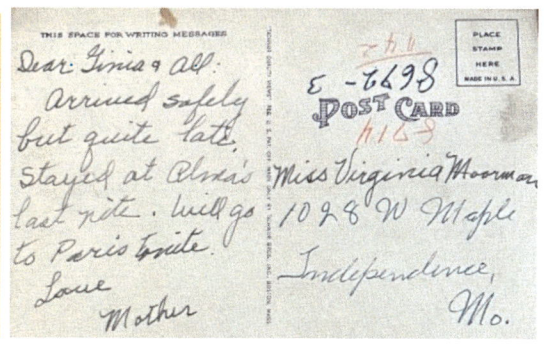

Postmark: none [after 1944?]

To: Miss Virginia Moorman, 1028 W Maple, Independence, Mo.

Dear Ginia & all: Arrived safely but quite late. Stayed at Alma's last night. Will go to Paris [Tennessee] tonight. Love, Mother

Editor Note: There is no date on this postcard, but it was likely after 1944 because that's when Kentucky Lake was created. Alma is probably Gela's cousin (see previous postcard) in Cottage Grove, Tennessee. Paris, Tennessee (where Gela was born and many family members lived), was about 12 miles to the southeast of Cottage Grove. It's not clear what the numbers (upside down in the upper right corner) indicate. This postcard was placed here (instead of in the 1940s section) because of its similarity to the postcard on the previous page and the family relationships.

~~~

Front: mountain wooded scene with picture of woman inset. 2121 HELEN HUNT'S GRAVE, SEVEN FALLS, COLORADO SPRINGS, COLORADO. Helen Hunt Jackson, famous as the author of "Ramona", lived in Colorado Springs and loved the mountains, especially South Cheyenne Cañon and at her dying wish was buried on a pine clad point overlooking her beloved Cañon and Colorado Springs.

Postmark: Colorado Springs, Colo., Aug 5, 1937, 5:30 PM; 1 cent stamp

To: Mrs. Oscar Moorman, 1028 W. Maple St., Independence, Mo

Manitou, Colorado

Dear Sis;

We are at Manitou got here Tuesday night all are well and not so tired as when we got here. Drove over six hundred sixty miles Tuesday. Hope you Oscar and the children are all well. Lots of love Eric [Cook]

Editor Note: This postcard is from Gela's older brother, Eric Cook. He is probably with his wife Altha and perhaps their daughter Peggy, 19. His son Don would be 21 and married at this time, so probably would not be with them. Manitou is about 6 miles from Colorado Springs, near Pikes Peak.

~~~

1940s

Left: Back: Enid, Eleanor; front: Virginia, Oscar, Gela, circa 1940s. Right: Gela, Virginia, first mother/daughter graduates of the Independence Sanitarium and Hospital School for Nurses, Independence, Missouri, 1941.

In January 1942, Gela wrote a letter to Virginia, who was attending school in Columbia, Missouri, about surgery that she'd had. It was probably an appendectomy, as Gela had gallbladder surgery in 1963. Gela was staying with her sister, Irma, during her recovery. Enid would have been 20 at this time and married to Marvin Wanbaugh. Eleanor would have been 13. The letter is transcribed in the book *Headlong in the Middle of a Wonderful Life*.

In April 1946, Gela and Oscar adopted David Kent Moorman, Virginia's child born in February 1946. Virginia served as an American Red Cross nurse in Hawaii during World War 2, 1944–1945, and returned to Missouri in December 1945. It's not known who David's biological father is.

~~~

Postcards, 1940s

Front: Portuguese dancers in costumes. **Editor Note:** Postcard illustration of people dancing at a local festival in the Minho region of Portugal by Portuguese artist Alberto Augusto de Sousa (1880-1961), circa 1935.

Postmark: illegible [1940/1941]; two 50 c Portugal stamps

To: Miss Virginia Moorman, 1413 West Van Horn, Independence—Missouri, U.S.A.

BILHETE POSTAL [POSTCARD]

PORTUGAL — Danças Regionais [regional dances] — MINHO [province in northwest Portugal]

May 17, 1940 Dear Virginia, Referring to my last letter, I must say you that I begged you send me that because it has not been published here, but I have just been informed that, owing to the delicate actual situation, the Censor here will not let I receive it. This picture represents a dance in our popular meeting. With my cumpsigento [accomplice] I am Cutech (?)

Editor Note: This street address was where Virginia was going to nursing school. The street Van Horn (named for Kansas City mayor Robert T. Van Horn) was renamed Truman Road in 1949 to honor President Harry S. Truman. It's unclear what Virginia might have sent that would have been censored.

~~~

Front: 15425 Seven Falls, So. Cheyenne Canon, Colorado Springs, Colorado, 267 Wooden and 20 Stone Steps Lead to the Top, a Height of 300 Feet. SEVEN FALLS, SOUTH CHEYENNE CANON Here are miles of massive walls of richly colored granite rising from the murmuring stream almost perpendicular to the sky above. Their bold and rugged pinnacles are split and broken by the never-ending battle with the elements; their lofty domes and towers standing alone and unsupported after centuries of upheaval and commotion, inconceivable to man, and in a magnificent and most impressive climax at the wonderful Seven Falls, where nature outdoes herself in a grand display of mighty cliffs and rushing waters.

Left: 2022 view of Seven Falls

Postmark: Manitou Springs, COLO, Nov 2, 1942, 4 PM; 1 cent stamp

To: Mrs. Oscar Moorman, 1028 W. Maple, Independence, Missouri

Hello. We have looked until our eyes are sore. Are visiting the Bales here. Love, Dema and Lester

~~~

Front: 903—Mt. Hood from Lost Lake, Oregon. **Editor Note:** Lost Lake is a picturesque natural lake sitting at the foot of Mount Hood, 25 miles southwest of Hood River. As early as the 1900s, the Mount Hood's view from the north lakeshore was used in postcards, calendars, and other souvenirs. The lake's surface area is 240 acres and the depth goes up to 175 feet. This is the second deepest lake in the Mt. Hood National Forest. Because the lake sits at an elevation of 3,000 feet above sea level and is fed by glacier creeks, the water is cold even at the peak of summer heat.

Left: 2022 view of Mt. Hood, Oregon.

Postmark: Portland, Oreg., Mar 18, 1944, 6 PM; 1 cent stamp

To: Mrs. Oscar Moorman, 1028 W. Maple, Independence, MO.

Hello Gella—Thought of you, so many times. We are having a wonderful trip. Spent Sunday with our boys, Helen & girls. Jim left Wed. Tues. we took a trip to the ocean, came back by way of camp and spent eve c ["with" as medical professionals write] John. Expect him to come and spent Sun c us. We plan to spend the day c relatives in Van Cover. Love Sarah

Editor Note: Unknown people mentioned in this postcard. Because the writer used "c" for "with," it might be someone who Gela knew from her work as a nurse at the hospital.

~~~

Front: 685—The Land of Sunshine, Fruits and Flowers, Southern California. Vistas of orange groves, palms, flower gardens and snow-capped mountains,—after the long trek across the desert, is the welcome to visitors upon arriving in Southern California.

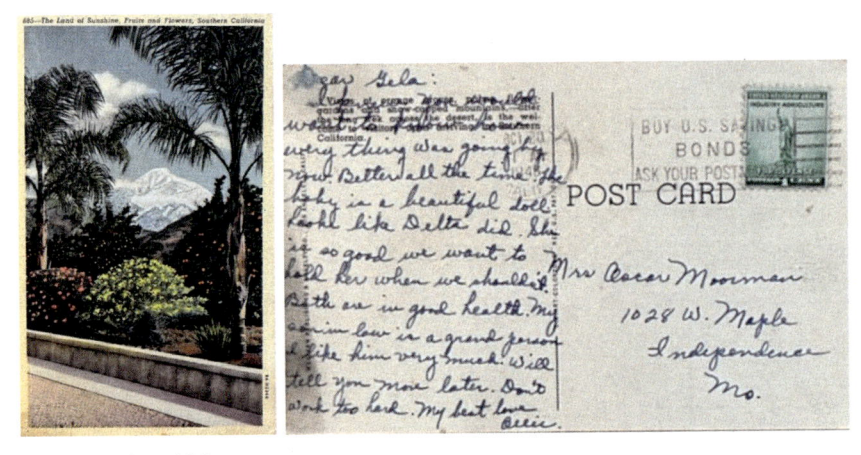

Postmark: Calif. Oct 20, 1948, 1 AM; 1 cent stamp

To: Mrs. Oscar Moorman, 1028 W. Maple, Independence, MO.

Dear Gela: I knew you would want to know how every thing was going by now. Better all the time. The baby is a beautiful doll. Looks like Delta did. She is so good. We want to hold her when we shouldn't. Both are in good health. My son in law is a grand person. I like him very much. Will tell you more later. Don't work too hard. My best love, Ollie.

Editor Note: Unknown people mentioned in this postcard. Unknown writer.

~~~

1950 US Census

1028 W. Maple, Independence, Jackson County, Missouri; Not on a farm, not on 3 acres or more

Oscar Moorman, head of household, white, male, 60, married, born in Missouri, worked 40 hours in the past week as a brickmason in construction for a private employer

Gela Moorman, wife, white, female, 56, married, born in Tennessee, homemaker, no work outside the home

David Moorman, son, white, male, 4, never married, born in Missouri

Steven Wanbaugh, grandson, white, male, 4, never married, born in Missouri

Virginia Moorman, head of household, white, female, 30, never married, born in Missouri, worked 48 hours in the past week as a nurse, private nursing

Dorothy Coffey, lodger, white, female, 30, divorced, born in Iowa, worked 40 hours the past week as a technician in a hospital

Editor Note: According to Steven Wanbaugh, he was probably living with his grandparents while his parents were in the process of a divorce. There was an upstairs apartment in this house where Virginia was living with her friend Dorothy Coffey.

~~~

Postcards, 1950s

Front: 1057 Wee Kirk of the Heather, Glendale, Calif. **Editor Note:** Between 1929 and 1930, Frederick A. Hansen created the Wee Kirk o' the Heather Chapel for Forest Lawn Memorial Park by copying the 17th century village church at Glencairn, Scotland, where Annie Laurie [born in 1682] worshipped.

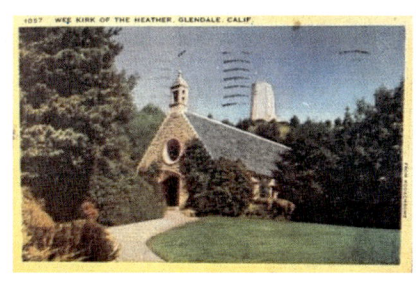

Postmark: Sunland, Calif., Jan 10, 1951, 5 PM; 1 cent stamp

To: Mr & Mrs. Oscar Moorman, 1028 W. Maple St., Independence, Mo.

Well, here we are had a fine trip and a wonderful driver. Its raining today which is much needed. We're goin to K.B. [Knott's Berry] Farm [in Buena Park, California] Sat. We still have a few places we want to see. Daisy Miller

Editor Note: There is a Daisy Lee Miller who lived at 715 N. Delaware, a few blocks from where Gela and Oscar lived on Maple. Daisy was born about 1895, so she would have been near Gela's age.

~~~

Front: View of Swimming Pool, Continental Guest Lodge, Phoenix, Arizona "It Costs No More at Continental." Lounge in our beautiful patio; swim in pure sparkling-clear water; play table tennis; enjoy shuffleboard games and dine in pleasant resort atmosphere at The CONTINENTAL Guest Lodge—56 Individual cottages, each with Telephone.

Postmark: Grand Canyon, Ariz., Jun 21, 1951, 8 PM, 1 cent stamp

To: Mrs. Moorman, 1026 [1028] Maple Ave., Independence, Mo

Having fine trip. Marilyn has never been west before. We have seen Hot Springs, Mexico, Grand Canyon & are now going to Boulder dam. Best regards, Lillian Farr

Editor Note: There is a Lillian S. Farr who lived at 1029 West Maple, Independence, Missouri. Lillian was born about 1893, so would have been about Gela's age. In 1951, she would have been 58. She had a daughter named Mary Lillian, who would have been about 15 at this time. If Lillian lived "across the street" on Maple, that might be why she got the wrong house number for Gela.

~~~

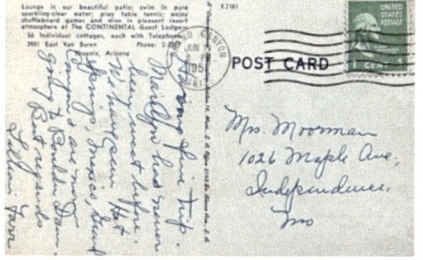

Front: Historic Mormon Landmarks at Nauvoo, Ill.

No. 1 JOSEPH SMITH HOMESTEAD—was originally a log house, built about 1826 by James Jones, an Indian agent, who sold it to Joseph Smith in 1839. The Prophet lived there until the spring of 1843, when he moved into the Mansion House.

NO. 2. MANSION HOUSE—Built in 1842 and 1843 through revelation. Home of the Prophet at the time he was killed at Carthage, Ill., June 27, 1844. Lumber sawed near LaCrosse, Wisc., and rafted down the river.

No. 3. THE NAUVOO HOUSE—A revelation was received Jan. 17, 1841, by Joseph Smith to build it and call it the Nauvoo House. An association was incorporated Feb. 15, 1841. It was never finished. Original plan was for three stories and basement.

Postmark: Nauvoo, Ill., Aug 5, 1952; 2 cent stamp

To: Mr Oscar Moorman, 1028 W. Maple Ave, Independence, Mo

Dearest Laddie [Oscar]: Sure wish you could have stayed for the classes promise to be more wonderful all the time. We just got back from town and will mail this I bought there in the A.M. <u>Love</u> Gela

Editor Note: The classes that Gela referred to might have been at an RLDS church reunion or a special conference held near Nauvoo, Illinois.

~~~

Front: 454 Fort Malden National Historic Park Museum, Amherstburg, Ontario, Canada.

Postmark: none [Mar 1951]

To: none [Gela Moorman]

Our doctor is here and we all came over to Canada to see what's what. Nothing much new. I won't be home until the end of next week—we are glad for the [medical] training but sooo homesick. [Virginia]

Editor Note: This note is from Virginia Moorman to her mother, Gela. Virginia often traveled for nursing work during the late 1940s and early 1950s. This was likely for one of those professional duties. She also wrote a postcard to her father, Oscar, dated Mar 1951. The image and the note are in the *Moorman Family Ancestor* book.

~~~

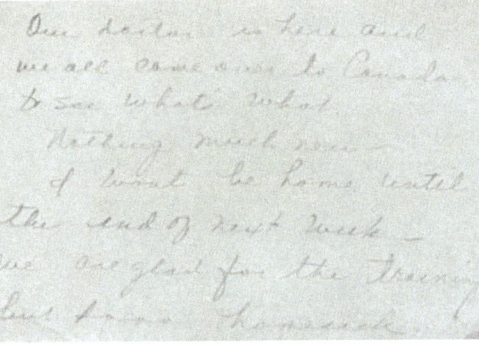

1952

Our dreams took shape.

We built a tower against the blue,

From which the Christmas chimes ring out

In carols, old and new.

"Will you make earth a place of peace?"

The songs keep asking you.

. . . Marcella Schenck

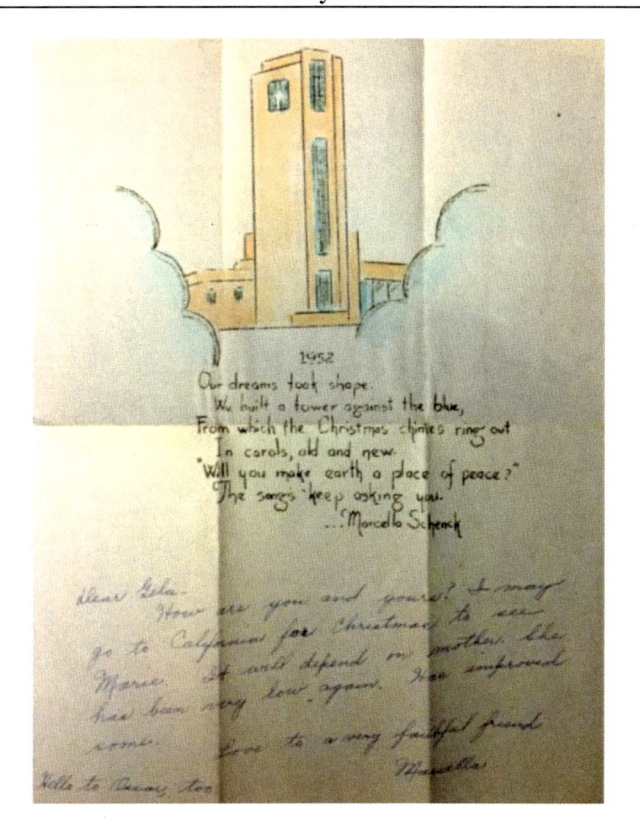

Dear Gela-

How are you and yours? I may go to California for Christmas to see Marie. It will depend on mother. She has been very low again. Has improved some.

Love to a very faithful friend, Marcella

Hello to Oscar, too.

Marcella Schenck to Gela Moorman. See 18 Dec 1923 postcard for details about Marcella. Marcella's mother, Laura Ellen Davis Needham Schenck, died 29 Jan 1953. Marcella died 22 Nov 1953 In Lamoni, Iowa, at age 66.

Marcella Nevada Schenck (1887-1953).

~~~

1960s–1970s

Gela and Oscar had lived at 1028 W. Maple, Independence, Missouri, during the 1920s until the 1950s. They relocated to Knob Noster, Missouri, where they lived until Oscar died in 1963. After that time, Gela stayed with her three daughters for various lengths of time and then resided in a nursing home in Dearborn, Missouri. She died in 1972 at the age of 79.

Left: Gela, unknown date. Middle: Gela holding Spanish moss, Florida, 1967.
Right: Oscar and Gela Moorman, Independence, Missouri, circa 1960s.

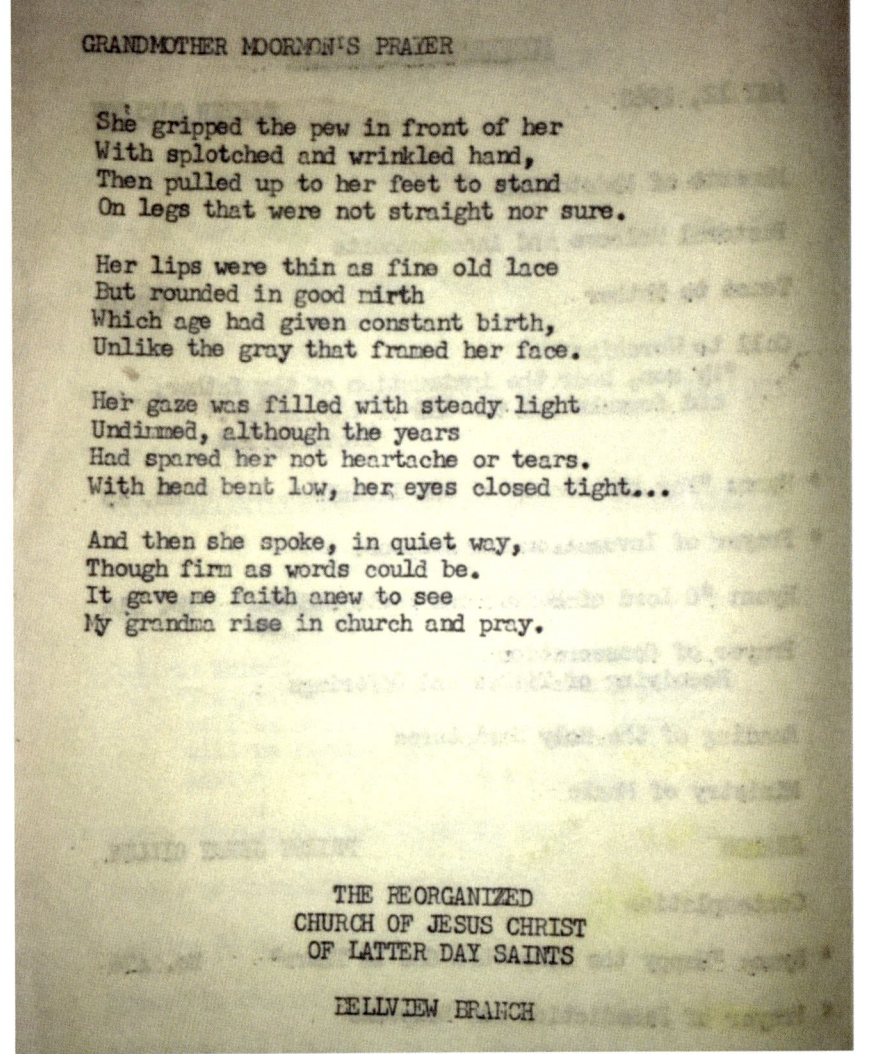

GRANDMOTHER MOORMON'S PRAYER

She gripped the pew in front of her
With splotched and wrinkled hand,
Then pulled up to her feet to stand
On legs that were not straight nor sure.

Her lips were thin as fine old lace
But rounded in good mirth
Which age had given constant birth,
Unlike the gray that framed her face.

Her gaze was filled with steady light
Undimmed, although the years
Had spared her not heartache or tears.
With head bent low, her eyes closed tight...

And then she spoke, in quiet way,
Though firm as words could be.
It gave me faith anew to see
My grandma rise in church and pray.

THE REORGANIZED
CHURCH OF JESUS CHRIST
OF LATTER DAY SAINTS

BELLVIEW BRANCH

Bellview Branch bulletin, Pensacola, Florida, 12 May 1968, Mother's Day.

Excerpts of Gela Moorman Letters

"As a small child I attended Foundry Hill where I was baptized. My Parents moved to Independence when I was still a child, and the memory of those growing up years near Stone Church are very precious to me.

At a district conference in Tennessee a baby, who had been ill for several days—Suddenly stopped breathing, lay perfectly still. Every one near thought him dead. He remained so for a couple of hours! But then, thru prayer and Administration [laying on of hands with a prayer by church ministers] he was restored, not only to life, but to health. He was fine when I saw him last.

When we first moved to Independence, I went to Columbian school.

One fine group [of people] was in New York City, where we lived a few years. Another in Knob Noster where we lived before I lost my beloved Husband.

There were no sacred happenings near Foundry [Tennessee] except my Baptism (at 8) in the Obion River—Bro I. N. Roberts did the baptizing & confirmation. A few comical things I do remember.

One Sunday, some of the dogs chased a big fat hog into the church. It ran squealing thru the church, dogs barking after it and on by the pulpit, and out the back door.

One day, just as services were well begun, the entire congregation got up and walked out. A fire in the neighborhood was going & did.

One late Spring Sunday after service a few of us girls went into the woods back of the Little church to find leaves to pop. It was nice then—but the next Sunday one of the girls had the distinct print of a leaf on her mouth as poison ivy pustules. So we knew she had chosen the wrong kind of leaf to pop!

One year for Childrens day, Mother made duplicate white dresses for the girls in my class. The only change was that each girl chose the colored baby ribbon to lace thru the eylet lace around the beritra [?] and sleeves of her dress! We did look sweet."

Gela's handwriting, 1970s.

Left: Gela holding Wendy Gates, Independence, Missouri, July 1970. Right: Gela, Missouri, 1970s.

IN MEMORY OF
Gela Lela Moorman
May 30, 1893
October 27, 1972

SERVICES
10:00 A. M. Monday
October 30, 1972
Speaks Chapel

OFFICIATING
Elder Lynn E. Smith
Elder F. Carl Mesle

MUSIC
Millicent Daugherty

INTERMENT
Knobnoster Cemetery
Knobnoster, Missouri

Gela Cook Moorman, 1893-1972, died age 79.

Summary of Maternal/Paternal First Generation

Tera and Myrtle Cook's Child

Kenneth Harold Cook

Born 1906.
Married Nancy M. Broadhead (1913-1969) in April 1943.
Child: Mary Emily Cook (1947-after 1969).
Died 1966. Kenneth and Nancy are buried at Mount Mora Cemetery, Saint Joseph, Missouri.

~~~

Berber and Grace Cook's Children

Berber and Grace Cook seated in front. Left to right: Mary and Doyle Cook, Leota and Joseph Pigg, Zelma and Scotty Cook, Betty Ballmer standing behind Grace, Ardyce and Charles Banker, Leona and R.B. Cook.

Raymond Berber "R.B." Cook

Born 1910.
Married Leona Louise Stoenner (1922-2005) on 5 Oct 1952 (Independence, Missouri).
Died 1965. R.B. and Leona are buried at Mound Grove Cemetery, Independence, Missouri.

Ardyce May Cook Banker

Born 1912.
Married Charles T. Banker (1914-1999) on 19 Jul 1947 (Independence, Missouri).
Died 1992. Ardyce and Charles are buried at Mound Grove Cemetery, Independence, Missouri.

Scott Elias Cook

Born 1914.
Married Zelma Lee McKendry (1916-1992).
Child: Thomas Scott Cook (1937-1951).
Child: Patricia Ann Cook Smith (1942-2014).
Died 2001. Scott and Zelma are buried at Mound Grove Cemetery, Independence, Missouri.

Leota Lucille Cook Pigg

Born 1916
Married Joseph Arthur Pigg (1914-1992) on 28 May 1936 (Kansas City, Missouri).
Child: Sylvia A. Pigg. (1937-alive 2021).
Child: Gary B. Pigg (1939-alive 2021).
Died 1986. Leota and Joseph are buried at Oak Grove Cemetery, Missouri.

Joseph Doyle Cook

Born 1923.
Married Mary Margaret Roark (1926-2010).
Child: Robert Doyle Cook (1947-2004).
Died 2008. Joseph and Mary are buried at Riverside National Cemetery, California.

Betty Lavelle Cook Ballmer

Born 1929.
Married Dallas Eldon Ballmer (1927-2006) on 31 Dec 1949 (Independence, Missouri).
Child: Vicki Harvey (after 1949-after 2004).
Child: Lisa Libich (after 1949- after 2004).
Child: Lori Luther (after 1949- after 2004).
Child: Scotti Pittman (after 1949- after 2004).
Child: Steve Ballmer (after 1949- after 2004).
Child: Dallas J. Ballmer (after 1949- after 2004).
Died 2004. Betty and Dallas died in Denham Springs, Louisiana. Unknown burial details.

~~~

Irma and Walter Stover's Children

Mildred, Pearl standing in front of Irma, Walter, Emma, and Clyde Stover, circa 1924.

Clyde Walter Stover

Born 1908.
Married Muriel Kirk Stover (1908-1996) on 16 Feb 1919.
Child: Shirley Louise Stover Winkinhofer (1936-2014).
Child: Betty Jeanne Stover (1939-1981).
Child: Robert "Bob" Kirk Stover (1946-2012).
Died 1979. Clyde and Muriel are buried at Floral Hills Cemetery, Kansas City, Missouri.

Ruby Emma Stover Willoughby

Born 15 Jan 1911.
Married Ammon H. Willoughby (1908-1966) about 1927.
Child: Paul Willoughby (10 Feb 1928-10 Feb 1928).
Died 10 Feb 1928. Emma and Ammon are buried at Mound Grove Cemetery, Independence, Missouri.

Mildred Louise Stover Van Artsdalen

Born 1912.
Married Russell Victor Van Artsdalen (1906-1981) on 14 Jan 1928.
Child: James William Van Artsdalen (1928-2019).
Child: Margaret Louise Van Artsdalen Flippin (1930-2018).
Child: Helen Francis Van Artsdalen Fitzwater (1933-2003).
Died 1969. Mildred and Russell are buried at Mount Washington Cemetery, Independence, Missouri.

Gela Pearl Stover Stevenson

Born 1916.
Married John William "Bill" Stevenson (1912-1972) on 5 Jun 1936.
Child: Viola P. Stevenson Berry Ressler (1938-2011).
Child: John Williams Stevenson Jr. (1947-2011).
Died 2011. Pearl and Bill are buried at Mound Grove Cemetery, Independence, Missouri.

Mary Elaine Stover Resch

Born 1925.
Married Clarence Albert "Bud" Resch Jr. (1924-2009) on 15 Mar 1946.
Child: Jim Resch (1949-alive 2021).
Child: Janice Resch Jones (1951-alive 2021).
Child: Patricia May Resch Taylor Cook (1953-alive 2021).
Died 1995. Elaine and Bud are buried at Mound Grove Cemetery, Independence, Missouri.

~~~

Eric and Altha Cook's Children

Donald William Cook

Born 16 Aug 1916.
Married Dorothy Adelyn Lanphear (1916-2005) on 8 Nov 1937.
Died 14 Jun 1964. Donald is buried at Mound Grove Cemetery, Independence, Missouri. Dorothy is buried at Brooking Cemetery, Raytown, Missouri, with her second spouse, Howard William Pollard.

Margaret "Peggy" L. Cook

Born 7 May 1918.
Died 2 Nov 2003. Peggy is buried at Mound Grove Cemetery, Independence, Missouri.

~~~

Gela and Oscar Moorman's Children

Virginia Merle Moorman

Born 7 Feb 1920 (Independence, Missouri).
Child: David Kent Moorman born 15 Feb 1946 (Kansas City, Missouri); died 16 Feb 1975 (Destin, Florida).
Married Anthony Joseph Zukowsky (1917; 1985) on 20 Apr 1951 (1028 W. Maple Avenue, Independence, Missouri), divorced 28 Feb 1955.
Child: Joni Merlene Zukowsky Dungan Wilson born 18 Mar 1953 (Independence, Missouri).
Child: Susan Jane Zukowsky Dungan Barnes born 4 Sep 1954 (Independence, Missouri).
Married Alma Lafayette Dungan (1908; 1972) on 31 May 1965 (Kansas City, Missouri).
Died 15 Dec 1997 (Crestview, Florida). Cremated.

Enid Eloise Moorman

Born 21 Mar 1921 (Independence, Missouri).
Married Marvin Leroy Wanbaugh (1920; 2004) on 11 Dec 1941 (Independence, Missouri); divorced.
Child: Steven Keith Wanbaugh born 29 Jan 1946 (Independence, Missouri).
Married Louis Burnette Cruce (1926; 2000) on 14 Sep 1956 (Independence, Missouri).
Child: Gregory Lance Cruce born 16 Oct 1957 (Independence, Missouri).
Child: Robin Michele Rieken Golden Cruce born 24 May 1960 (Independence, Missouri).
Died 25 Feb 2003 (Independence, Missouri).

Eleanor Rose "Mickey" Moorman

Born 8 Apr 1928 (Edgewater, New Jersey).
Married Bertrand Homer Sartwell (1927; 1982) on 5 Feb 1949 (Independence, Missouri), divorced.
Child: Teresa Denise Sartwell Ewbanks Rathbun born 27 Sep 1949 (Independence, Missouri).
Child: Dennis Charles Sartwell born 2 May 1951 (Independence, Missouri).
Child: Laure Kay Sartwell Smith Davis born 14 May 1955 (Independence, Missouri).
Child: Lisa Beth Sartwell Hensley born 20 Jul 1963 (Independence, Missouri).
Died 15 Jul 1987 (Independence, Missouri). Cremated.

~~~

Made in the USA
Columbia, SC
29 November 2022